"FLY!"

By

Lex Gillette

ISBN: 978-1-951503-07-9 (Ebook)
ISBN: 978-1-951503-06-2 (Paperback)

Published by Authorsunite.com

Contents

Author's Note

The doctor's words hit like a hammer. "Elexis will never see again."

Pretty tough news for anyone – especially for an eight-year-old boy. Little did I know that traumatic event would eventually help me focus on my life and goals more clearly than any set of eyes.

Though what follows lays out my life, the primary intent of this book is not to serve as an autobiography. I hope what you read will open your mind to new possibilities, fresh opportunities, and uninhibited potential.

I want you to enjoy the stories...

...stories where you will meet the very special people who helped me shape my approach to life...

...stories of my experiences in Paralympic sport...

...stories of triumph – and disappointment...

...stories that may bring on a smile, laughter, or tears.

I want you to learn about me – about yourself – and about the beauty of the world we all occupy. It is my sincere hope that you will take something from these pages – my ideas and observations – and apply them in your own journey.

Anything significant involves others. A lot of people have helped me. And I want to make sure I acknowledge them with appreciation, respect, and affection.

My godfather, Troy Croom, loves to say, "Give people their roses while they can still smell them." Good advice, but I would be absolutely broke if I tried to purchase long-stems for everyone who has impacted my life.

I hope this book will serve as a suitable substitute.

If I've learned one thing, it's that sight might not determine our success but a vision will. There are millions of people walking across the planet with 20/20 eyesight but when it comes to "vision," they cannot see a thing.

This book is about the people who saw something in me – and who helped me to find it within myself.

Gravity is an undeniable force of Nature. It pulls us down – it locks us to the Earth. But "vision" is gravity's Kryptonite.

Every single person can levitate – we can all rise higher – we can all move toward the sky. If we have a vision...

...we can all fly!

Elexis "Lex" Gillette

Prologue

The long-jump has been part of the Olympic Games since their inception in 776 BC. Although the rules for modern competition differ significantly, the event still represents an important part of the spectacle.

Every four years, men and women hurtle down a runway towards a take-off board located 1 to 3 meters from the closer end of the landing area. The soles of a jumper's shoe cannot exceed a thickness of 13 millimeters. Spikes are allowed.

Competitors can position location markers in as many as two places along the runway. After sprinting down the runway, a jumper's farthest point of contact with the 20-centimeter-wide take-off board must be behind the board's leading edge. If so much as a toenail crosses the line, it's a foul and the jump does not count. Competitors land in the sand of the landing area – a space whose width can be from 2.75 to 3.0 meters.

Somersaults are prohibited.

Imagine what it would be like. You take your place at the far end of the runway. You know you have one minute to begin your approach after your shoe touches the track.

You have your routine down. You position yourself just so at the end of the runway and visualize your soon-to-be successful leap. Everything you've ever learned over years of training and hundreds of practice jumps flashes through your mind in rapid sequence.

You imagine your lead foot hitting the board – the board you know is there through your peripheral vision. To stare at the board means your head will be lowered at the take-off, thus reducing speed and, ultimately, distance. Worse, focusing on the board might bring about a foul, a lost opportunity. You sense where the board is; it's not a soccer ball; it won't move.

You visualize your perfect take-off: one leg up, then the next rising to meet it, a bicycle motion in the air, then an exquisitely clean landing where you pitch forward because they will measure from the board to the spot first touched by any part of your body.

It's time. You are ready.

The crowd grows still in anticipation and the spectators sense the coming fury of your attempt. They grow louder and louder. They know you are preparing to launch – to defy gravity – to attempt to fly.

Now, just as you take your first step, the initial movement forward that will be followed by ever-increasing acceleration... just before you push off your back foot to begin your charge down the 30 to 40 meters of rubberized surface – *close your eyes and keep them shut throughout the entire competition.*

Welcome to the world of Lex Gillette.

Out of Sight – Never Out of Mind

When I was born, I could see.

I grew up in Raleigh, the capital city of North Carolina.

I remember the green of the grass and the Carolina blue of the sky.

I've seen roses and dogwoods in bloom, the glory of a sunset, the green-gray gloom of a southern thunderstorm. I remember the blur of the spokes of a bicycle flying down the street and the blistering beauty of a cardinal – our state bird.

I can still see the neighborhood where I used to play, the friends I had, and my school. There are lots of things I remember.

But, for the life of me, I cannot remember what my mother looked like. Baffles me a little and bothers me a lot. I recall certain characteristics. She had very long, black hair, a river of onyx running across her shoulders, but her face remains fuzzy, like something from a dream.

I grew up in an apartment complex called Crown Court. Crown Court off of Wake Forest Road in Raleigh. Riding down the sidewalk on my bike, on the right-hand side like I was supposed to, I remember passing McDonald's, then reaching a bridge. The

1

name of whatever body of water the bridge crossed escapes me and isn't important enough to research but as soon as we traversed the bridge, we headed to the Miami Subs Grill on the right-hand side of the street. When we went a little farther and crossed the road, we ran right into Snoopy's, world's best hotdogs.

Ma and I always had adventures. We went everywhere together. I loved it when she took me to Snoopy's for a hotdog with chili, ketchup, and mustard, a lemonade or a fruit punch and a big helping of French fries – they had the crinkle-cut kind. Now, I am a French fry connoisseur. No, I am a fries snob. I consider French fries to be a free-standing food group. I love them all: golden and "supersized" from McDonald's, waffle cuts from Chick-fil-A, and Bojangles' seasoned fries. But the ones from Snoopy's were grease-infused perfection. Crispy as fried chicken on the outside, soft as a marshmallow on the inside. They were lightly-salted and always piping-hot. I could eat those crunchy fries three times a day, every day!

Crown Court was 50 to 75 yards right down the street from Snoopy's. Turn right at the entrance and once you wrestled your bike up to the top of the hill, you were at our apartment on the left-hand side. It was the last apartment in that complex, the last one at the end of the building on the first floor, first level.

We lived in a decent-sized neighborhood. Getting out of the car, you stepped onto the sidewalk, turned to the left and when the sidewalk almost reached the grass, you turned right. At the top of the third step, you turned to the left and walked five or six paces.

Ninety degrees right, another half-dozen steps and you reached our front door.

You entered directly into the living room. A few paces forward took you into the dining room – four to six more, depending on your stride, and you were in the kitchen. The back yard lay just outside the kitchen. The other side of the dining room led to our bathroom sandwiched between our bedrooms. From the doorway of the bathroom, the toilet and sink stood on the right wall; the bathtub ran along the left-hand wall.

You learn to memorize floor plans when you are blind. If you think the toilet's on the left, when you go to sit, you're in for an unpleasant surprise. Hitting the bottom of a porcelain tub hurts, even when you're a little kid. As you get taller, the fall gets longer.

"Carpet art" of *The Last Supper* hung on the dining room wall. I can remember a fuzzy image of Jesus and the Twelve but my mother's face is a blur.

Despite the picture, Ma had good taste. The china cabinet in the dining room was always perfectly arranged. I liked how the afternoon sun gleamed off the plates, cups and saucers.

My mom was meticulous when it came to our home; it was always spotless.

**

Although I "officially" lost my sight when I was eight, the story started a lot earlier. Ma noticed I was standing really close to the television as a three-year-old. It was about time for my check-up, so she mentioned the issue to the doctor.

I had a cataract. Imagine, a toddler with a cataract in his left eye.

The procedure went well, but while I was recovering, I suffered a detached retina in the same eye. Two operations later, I lost all sight in my left eye.

But it was all good. I still had one good one.

Today, you regularly see kids wearing glasses. But I was pretty young and my glasses looked like the bottoms of Cheerwine bottles. (Yes, you must be from the Carolinas to understand Cheerwine.) A few kids poked fun here and there, but I wasn't bullied. I could take it and I never hesitated to dish it out.

I could still see the world – my world – Crown Court.

There was a ledge. I can still get you there. Step out of the parking space closest to our apartment, walk to the end of the sidewalk where it meets the grass, turn right, walk up the three stairs, then left. One more immediate left and you are standing three feet above the grass.

I loved to fling myself off the ledge. I wanted to fly, so I'd run, leap, then spread my arms like wings. In my heart, I felt – I knew – that one day my feet would not touch the ground, that I would defy the law of gravity and soar through the air.

I hit that patch of grass – every single time.

But I'm still trying.

And, I am getting closer.

**

I loved catching fireflies. We call them "lightning bugs" in the Carolinas. I was good at it. I cupped my hands – tight enough to secure the little critters, but always careful to avoid crushing them. My prisoners went into jars - complete with holes in the lids.

At night, I sat in my room and watched the glass shimmer as the "taillights" flickered on and off. Sometimes I put dirt and grass in the jars - little homes for my pets. I made sure they had food and stuff from the kitchen. Hey, I was a kid. How was I supposed to know that fireflies didn't eat bread?

On warm summer evenings, my mom sat on the ledge, my launch pad, and watched me to make sure I was okay. She sat and I did typical kid stuff. She tried to act like she was doing something else - reading a magazine or a book or sipping sweet tea, but I never doubted she was carefully watching every move I made.

I can still see the sunsets, how the sky went from orange to brown like slowly burning toast. I ran and spun like a top; I rolled in the grass and played with my friends. All the while, my mom occupied a perfectly good ledge and never jumped a single time.

**

Life had a rhythm - a routine. I came from school, did my homework, then, if everything was okay with my mother, went outside to play with my friends until dinner. Nothing seemed to be different when I got home. I did my usual, finished my homework, asked and received permission, and ran around for an hour or so before coming inside. Dinner was just like always - delicious and overflowing with conversation about my day. I must have led a very interesting young life, because my mother always had lots of questions and I had lots of answers.

Bath-time came and I very dutifully went in to get clean.

Uh oh.

Things looked strange. Well, some things were the same. I was sitting in the tub and scrubbing myself with a washcloth, just like always. But the water looked different. It wasn't, "Wow, I must have been really dirty" different.

It was murky – cloudy.

I looked at the bathroom lights.

They were faint, like the electrical current to the house had suddenly been cut in half.

I hopped out of the tub, toweled off, hoisted myself onto the small counter, and stared into the mirror at the faint image of a reflection I knew was mine. It didn't look a thing like me. For the first seven years of my life, I had grown accustomed to seeing a young boy with big brown eyes, dark skin, and short black hair. Now, the face was a muddy smudge. It looked like my reflection was slowly melting off the glass.

A high-pitched "Ma!" spilled from my quivering lips and I heard footsteps rounding the corner. "Ma, something is wrong with my eyes. Everything looks really blurry."

My mom cradled my chin and tilted my head upward to look into my eyes. A few tears began to run down my cheek.

"I don't see anything wrong, Elexis, but we can take some eyedrops and clean your eyes. Maybe you have a little soap in there." She left the bathroom and returned quickly with a small bottle. She tilted my head back and dripped the solution into my eyes. Moisture streamed from the corners of my eyes, more my tears than the drops, to be sure.

My mom took some tissue and dabbed my face. "Let's see if that works honey. It's getting late, so you may just need to get a little rest. I'm thinking everything should be better by the morning."

The drops did make my eyes feel better, but my sight was still blurred. The two of us walked toward the door and I saw the faint motion of my mom's arm reaching toward the wall. The bathroom went dark behind us as we moved into my bedroom.

I went to sleep with the calm assurance of an eight-year old. Everything would be okay in the morning. I had no idea what was going on but a few things crossed my mind.

Am I okay?

Are my eyes going to look funny?

Are people going to pick on me - more?

And, the big one...

Am I going blind?

Morning came and nothing changed. I looked at the world through a dingy film. Even though everything was blurry, I was still breathing. According to my mother's rules, that qualified me to get dressed and go to school.

I don't remember anything about the day except one thing: my mom had to come get me. She'd gotten a message from the school: "Elexis is not himself today. He keeps bumping into things..."

**

The examination revealed I had a detached retina again, this time in my right eye. One emergency operation later, everything seemed back to normal. While things weren't crystal-clear at first, I could make out images and the like. That was a good thing. I felt better about my chances.

Over the next few weeks, I had to wear an eye patch. Not my idea of a good time. (Ironically, many years later, I graduated from East Carolina University, home of – you guessed it – The Pirates.)

Eventually, they let me dump the Blackbeard look and wear a protective shield over my eye. It was clear and protected my eye from dirt and anything that might cause an infection.

Things were looking up until, one day, my vision veered off into "Blurryland" again. The doctor told me I had detached the same retina again.

Another operation, another apparent success. Although my eye was sensitive to light when I was released, at least I could see. Despite two surgical procedures in the span of two months, I felt pretty good.

Then the snowball started downhill and the mess grew progressively bigger and more threatening.

First bandages over my eye. Then, another clear, protective shield. Then, blurred vision, another trip to the doctor, and ta-da! - another detached retina.

I might have been a tough kid but I was still a kid. Going back to the hospital, putting on another ridiculous, rear-end exposing gown, and wearing a very-not-cool wrist band were bad enough. But all those signs pointed to the same destination: the operating room.

I hated the ride down the hall. I hated watching the blur of the lights as they slid by overhead. I hated the cold steel of the hard table. I hated the hands that slipped the gas mask over my diminutive face. I hated the noxious, sticky-sweet smell of the anesthetic. I hated the countdown. I even hated the sound of my own name: "Elexis, can you count backward from one hundred? We want to see how far you can go."

They must have thought I didn't remember this from the last time. I remembered every detail – and I knew the farthest I ever got was "97...96...95."

Over the string of ten operations, I did not start loving those things – not even a little. Sometimes, I grabbed the doorframe of my hospital room, screaming and crying, and the nurses had to pry my fingers loose; sometimes I lied and told the doctor I had to go to the bathroom just to delay the start of the next procedure. If I could have climbed out of the window, I would have scaled the wall like Spiderman. Anything so they would not wheel me down that antiseptic hall again.

**

After the tenth operation (I'd endured thirteen starting at three years old), Dr. Brooks McKewen talked to my mother.

"Ms. Gillette, we have tried everything. Your son will eventually go blind. I am sorry, but there is nothing else we can do."

Again, the questions rattled around in my head.
So, now what?
Can I play my video games?
Ride my bike?
Will I recognize my friends? See my mother's hair?
Can I still go get a dog at Snoopy's?
What about flying off the ledge?
What's next?

Well, what was next was routine. School, homework, playing with friends, dinner, bath, then bedtime – and one more thing. I woke up every morning seeing a little less than I did the day before.

**

It had always been us two – my mom and me. Every day started with my mom. Most mornings I would wake to the faint sounds of music playing from her bedroom, then roll over like I hadn't heard anything and try to snatch a few more precious moments of sleep. Then, "Elexis, it's time to get up." She'd let me lie there for a little longer, but after a while, she took matters into her own hands.

The room light would come on, a sleep-shattering burst of illumination. You know how it is when you get that first glimpse of light in the morning. It's absolutely painful, but every day I had to squint a little less because the light wasn't as bright.

"Elexis, get up. You're going to be late to school."

And every day ended with the two of us on our knees next to my bed. Our prayers didn't last as long as the ones in church – the ones where people called to "Sweet Jesus" for help. Those prayers surely did not go on for as long as I imagined, but to my eight-year-old mind, once the preacher got people to prayin', it was a good idea to get comfortable.

My mom made sure I was attentive and respectful in church. But even if I might have snoozed on occasion, I knew prayer time was when people asked for things: help with finances, healing from "the rheumatism" (whatever that was), "safety for my boy" (no one ever prayed much for "my girl" – girls must have been tougher). I knew what I wanted to ask in my prayers. I wanted my eyes to be okay. I wanted to see normally again.

But, every night, when I hit my knees, I regurgitated the same little rhyme: "Now I lay me down to sleep, I pray the Lord my soul to keep, and if I die before I wake, I pray the Lord my soul to take. Amen."

Mom and I embraced. "I love you, son," she said. I squeezed her mightily. "I love you, too, Ma."

I slid into my bed and pulled the covers up to my chin. I couldn't help but notice the faint glimmer of light seeping into my room at the corner of the window where the curtain was not completely closed. For now, I could still glimpse a little part of the world, but how much longer would it last? In a matter of months, I'd gone from seeing the crisp, clearly-defined edges of life to barely recognizing the reflection staring back at me from the mirror. My last conscious thought was always, *"Maybe it'll be better in the morning."*

Seemingly just after I drifted off to sleep, a voice called to me, "Elexis?" I rolled over and buried my head under the pillow. "Elexis, wake up. How's everything looking today?"

I poked my head from underneath the blanket and pillow and gazed at the graying, deteriorating world I'd seen the day before. The view did not improve even with vigorous eye rubbing.

"It's the same, Ma," I said.

Every day, the same ritual. Every day, I made my morning report without passion. "Still blurry, Ma."

"Maybe we should go to the doctor."

Nothing good ever came from seeing the doctor. The way things were going, the next time I wandered into a doctor's office, someone was going to jab a hypodermic needle into my eye.

No way!

"Ma, I can see well enough to go to school today," I said.

"Are you sure? I don't know." Her voice sounded a little uneasy.

"Yes, I'll be fine," I responded. Anything, even a day of wandering around and hitting a good portion of an ever-darkening school with my face beat the heck out of a visit to any doctor's den of torture.

Then, one day, when I woke up, I couldn't see anything at all.

Reality hit me in the teeth. I couldn't play my video games because I couldn't see Mario, Yoshi, Luigi, King Koopa, or any of the other characters. I couldn't see my neighborhood. I couldn't see my mother.

I couldn't even see Carpet Jesus.

Somewhere in the back of my mind, I'd known the doctors, who were very good and very kind, were not going to be able to make everything all better.

The doctors and nurses were compassionate and competent, but they weren't magicians. After over a dozen operations, I think I had subconsciously been preparing to live in the darkness. I'd heard, "no change," "detached retina," "impact on his vision," "limitations" for so long, that when someone finally threw the power switch to my eyes to "off," I wasn't exactly shocked.

I might even have been a little relieved.

**

Words fail me when I try to give my mom proper credit. Whatever I am today results from her tender, yet demanding nature. Ma absolutely did not play.

Before I lost my sight, I had chores: cleaning my room, washing the dishes, taking out the trash, helping with washing the clothes, cleaning the bathroom. I was expected to complete my assignments on time and thoroughly. If a food-encrusted pan landed in the drying rack, it went back in the sink where I scrubbed it again.

Once I lost my sight, I had the same chores. And that pan kept coming back! There's some security in that. When my athletic career ends, I can always get a job as a professional-grade dish washer.

Good manners were never an option. I ate properly, sat straight at the table, and addressed people as "sir" and "ma'am" (old school, folks – old school). One more thing: I looked everyone in the eye.

Kids tend to shy away from adults. Looking up at someone who is towering over you is both intimidating and uncomfortable. But my mother insisted. "Elexis, when someone speaks to you, always look in the direction of the voice. Give them your undivided attention."

The concept proves difficult enough for an average kid – imagine what happens to a child when he loses his sight. For some inexplicable reason, as my eyesight faded, my embarrassment increased, like I'd done something wrong. Ma simply blew my impending humiliation out of the water. "You may not be able to see them, but they can see you. Give them your full respect."

My mother trained me to be independent and capable; I can live alone and take care of myself. My room remains tidy and clean most of the time. If the need arises, I can man a vacuum cleaner with the best of 'em.

And, like any young boy, starvation always seemed just around the corner. I was hungry and I wanted to eat. But, when the food hit the table, picking it up and shoving it in my mouth never crossed my mind – not with my mother sitting there.

"Elexis, use your knife and fork like a proper young man."

Close your eyes and try it some time. I bet you stab yourself in the cheek at least twice. But I learned, and I am better for it.

Nothing ever happened at my house by chance; everything had been carefully planned out, right up to its location.

My mom suffers from a vision impairment as well. At eighteen, she was diagnosed with glaucoma. While she has sight – she wears a significant pair of glasses. To reduce dependence on others, she picked our location to minimize the distances we had to cover. We lived close to grocery and retail stores, fast food places, the park, and – for times when we had to go a longer way – the bus stop. My mom remains a meticulous and precise woman.

**

We played ball and other games, Ma and I did. I get whatever athletic ability I have from her and her side of the family. She loved to come outside for a game of catch. We particularly enjoyed bouncing a neon green ball back and forth. It was about the size of a basketball – we got it from K-Mart – you remember, the store kept them in giant cages and kids threw them all over the stores. They were feather-light and bounced like crazy! We had a great time.

Some guys cringed when their mothers attempted sports.

I beamed. Ma was a boss!

When it came time to get serious, we got serious. I never got a pass, especially after I went blind. In the fall of every year, the school sent home mid-term reports. While not official report cards, they gave an indication of how I was performing academically. One year, in October, I grinned as I handed over my mid-term to my mother. I was especially pleased with my "97" in math – always one of my best subjects. Bada-bing! This was going to be great!

The house grew eerily quiet.

"Elexis, I see you have a 'zero' for two missing homework assignments in math. Can you explain those?"

"Ah, well...you see the 97, right?"

"Yes, but I am far more interested in knowing what you were doing on the days when you were supposed to be doing your homework."

I wanted to mention the 97 again, but thought better of it.

"You *will* be doing your homework every afternoon, correct?"

"Yes, ma'am."

I didn't bring home any more "zeros."

My mother did not tolerate un-swept corners, either in my room, or in my mind.

**

One of the places my mother's unbridled, amazing affection shone brightest was in my relationship with my dad. I have a number of friends whose fathers weren't around. They still carry a lot of anger and resentment about their absentee dads, and I get it.

I feel differently.

My mom would not let it happen. She made sure I had some contact with my father. She put whatever feelings she had aside to ensure I had a relationship with my dad – that speaks volumes to her character and her commitment to my best life.

Not everyone is like that.

I stayed out of "grown folks" business. What happened between my parents wasn't any of my concern. Dad was a Marine – stationed for most of the time at Camp Lejeune, 128 miles from Raleigh – near Jacksonville, NC. I spent time in the summers with my father's family and with my dad. Sure, I had way more contact with my mom's side of the family, but my dad's branch was just as important. They're all family and I love each and every one of them.

Our custom was for my mom and me to spend Christmas at her mother's home in La Grange, NC. Everyone was there: aunts, uncles, cousins – everyone from Mom's side. It was a huge celebration. Then, I went to visit my sister, my dad, and my Aunt Delores for another blow out. Christmas was fantastic!

In 2009, a day or so after the Big Day, I headed to Sumter, SC. Later in the evening, my dad and I went outside. By that time, I'd started competing pretty seriously, and I was enjoying some success.

Dad told me how "super-proud" he was of me. I'd always known he was supportive – I'd heard how he liked to brag about me – but it was great to hear those words from his mouth. Yes, I would have loved for him to have been around. There's something special about a bond between a father and a son, but life happens, and we can't control everything. We can only control how we react.

Sumter lies about two-and-a-half hours from Charlotte, NC. I figured my travels would take me to the Queen City at some point down the road. My dad said he wanted to come up when I was there – to hang out and grab some food.

Sounded like a plan to me. It was a great Christmas.

On March 1, 2010, I had just finished a photo shoot. Tired and sweaty, I got ready to take a shower. The phone rang – it was my sister. I decided I would call her back when I was finished. Right before I stepped into the hot water, she called again. I ignored it. After I toweled off, I noticed she had called a third time. She never blows up my phone, so I figured she had something on her mind.

Our dad had been involved in an automobile accident. He'd been killed on impact.

My father was gone, but I know he was proud of me, and that simple fact is enough for me.

Still, the Rock remains – my mother – the Mission Control that launched my life and the source of my continuing strength. Like everything else, Ma's image disappeared into the darkness around me many years ago.

Her impact and presence remain. She may be out of sight but she will never be out of mind.

Grab Your Cane...

You'd think someone would notice a blind man going the wrong way on an escalator. But in Las Vegas, people have other things on their mind.

I was sweating like I was in a sauna, stepping and climbing, and getting nowhere. Connie kept telling me the escalator was the only way to cross Las Vegas Boulevard, one of the busiest streets in the country. So, I kept right on a-climbing.

**

My "mobility cane." White with a red tip. You've certainly seen one. By the time my orientation and mobility specialist, Mr. John Higgins, put one in my hand, I had probably seen one, too, but I don't remember. What I do recall very vividly is my complete revulsion over the thought of using it.

I'm not an old man. I don't need any senior discount cards. I move and walk all on my own. I do not need a cane!

But I was wrong. I needed it like a fish needs water.

Every student wants recognition, but, no one wants to be different. So, as soon as I learned the layout for Carroll Middle School, I ditched the cane. I moved through the halls pretty well. I knew how many steps it took to walk down a particular hallway. I could find my classes, the library, the cafeteria, and the bathroom. Think about it. If you had to, you could probably get around your home or office pretty well with your eyes closed.

But as soon as I left the building, like in a social situation, I had a problem. My friends saw me moving so effortlessly every day, that they sometimes forgot I was blind. When we got into an unfamiliar environment, my buddies sometimes walked off and left me behind.

"Hey! Hey! I need a little help." That wasn't too embarrassing. I had to verbalize what I needed – to admit I could not see a blooming thing.

Mr. Higgins, soft-spoken and very educated, eased me into cane work. He showed me how to use it, not so much as an extension of my arms, but as a substitute for my eyes. We started working together when I was in grade school and he continued to teach me about navigation all the way through my high school days.

He liked to work with "wicker sticks" – small, 5-to-6-inch pop-up tabs with adhesive bottoms. Before I went on an excursion, Mr. Higgins made a map of the "objective," positioning the sticks on a piece of braille paper (thicker than the normal kind and firm enough to hold the sticks in place). Mr. Higgins had written the street names on the map in braille. I'd run my hands across the tactile map, which was the layout where I would be walking.

"This is Morgan. This is Hillsborough."

After we discussed everything, we'd go on a little adventure. Before I got out of the car, we'd review the plan.

"All right, Elexis. Your job is to get from where we are parked to TJ Cinnamons." One of my favorite places

- a local joint in Raleigh where they had incredible cinnamon rolls. I particularly liked the "cini-minis" - a cluster of half a dozen, miniature confections. The plate was always warm, the dough always soft, and the sticky icing always thick enough to have been applied with a trowel.

Heaven in my mouth.

The instructions continued. "You're going to have to cross these three streets. Along the way, you'll encounter all sorts of driveways. About halfway there, you'll pass two businesses. Lots of cars going in and out of them. Once you get to the destination, we'll have a cinnamon roll... or six."

With my cane in my right hand, I exited the car and took off, the map made of wicker sticks etched in my brain. Mr. Higgins followed 25-30 feet behind to make sure everything went okay. I slid my cane left to right, making sure there wasn't anything in my path and ensuring I stayed on the sidewalk.

It was important to keep the cane moving. Lingering too long on my right could lead to my running into the telephone pole on my left. After a while, I used the cane like a bloodhound uses its nose - to know where I was, what was around, and what was coming.

**

Mr. Higgins helped to unravel the mysteries of the darkness surrounding me. As soon as I learned the basics, my "cane lessons" took the form of excursions - learning to move more freely through the community, going to the mall, and similar outings.

Mr. Higgins excelled at his job. Thanks to him, I've boarded flights to Denver, Washington DC, Australia, Japan, England, Finland – wherever. I never have any concern about my ability to get to the right gate at the right time without falling on my face. The lessons Mr. Higgins taught and the countless steps we put in around Athens Drive High School and the rest of Raleigh continue to play a huge role in my maneuverability.

I can travel, shop for clothes, go to the grocery store and get the right foods. Do not for a minute think I do it all by myself all the time. No, one of the most valuable lessons Mr. Higgins taught me was how to ask for help. Sales personnel, counter attendants at airports, and restaurant servers want to help. Sometimes they are reluctant to ask me what I need for fear of hurting my feelings or simply not knowing how to assist me.

Because of Mr. Higgins, I never hesitate to say, "Excuse me, but could you give me a hand here?"

After I lost my sight, I battled against insecurity. Growing up – being a teenager – dealing with a maturing physique and the other traumas of youth are daunting enough. Wondering how people were going to react to me made everything worse.

"What's wrong with that kid?"

Just so you know, people who are blind can't see but most of us can hear just fine.

But, having people like Mr. Higgins in my corner was huge. He taught me how to approach a stranger for assistance. In a restroom: "Hey, could you point me to the paper towels?" At the Post Office: "I'd like to mail this letter; would you mind helping me purchase a stamp?"

The list is endless.

None of those things seems very difficult but, to a newly-blind nine - ten - thirteen-year-old, they are nearly impossible. Remember, no one remotely suspected I would become a Paralympic athlete who would travel the world. Mr. Higgins never once suggested I might become a motivational speaker. He just wanted me to live a meaningful life, to be a happy, successful human being – independent – someone who could use public transportation, get around any school or neighborhood, travel safely and shop with confidence.

That dear man lay the world at my feet and said, "Go on, kid, take what you want!" He ignited a fire inside me and promoted a realistic belief that I could do anything.

Mr. Higgins gets a lot of credit, but everything positive for me started at home. My mom never quit, never let me wallow in self-pity, never let me skip my schoolwork, never let me give up.

All of which leads to Las Vegas, Connie, and the wrong-way escalator.

**

In June of 2017, I competed at the National Championships at UCLA's Drake Stadium. Well, "competed" is a nice word. It implies I did something positive. The only good thing I did was show up.

The event served as the qualifying competition for athletes who wanted to go to the World Championships in London in July. A lot of people turned out to watch me. I don't know if they were disappointed, but I surely was.

I did not have "it." My timing was slightly off. My legs felt fine, but I didn't jump as far as usual. I never hit the take-off board squarely. By the end of the event, I was not sure I was going to be invited to go to the United Kingdom.

I was bummed.

I needed to do something to get my mind off of the long-jump – something to relax – something to unwind. So, I did what anyone else would have done.

On Sunday afternoon, once the competition was over, I jumped on a plane to Vegas.

One of my buddies was celebrating his twenty-fifth birthday. I packed an overnight bag – I can travel pretty light when I need to – and headed to LAX to catch my Spirit flight. As soon as I landed, it was "on."

There were four of us. I'd been to Vegas numerous times, but the other guys were rookies. I took the lead in showing them the ropes. We had a great time – food, drink, laughter, and stories.

We were all in a good mood. It was time to "hit the Strip." We got dressed and made our way outside. When we reached the Bellagio, we were all amazed. The stores at that place were astounding: Gucci, Prada, Dior, Hermes, Harry Winston, Armani, Omega, Tiffany – and we hit them all. Fabulous merchandise.

And, of course, no high-end window-shopping trip is complete without a stroll through Louis Vuitton.

A little confession here: I have a thing about backpacks. A good backpack keeps me hands-free, plus, I have ready access to all my stuff. In the Louis Vuitton store, one of my buddies called to me.

"Hey, Lex, check this out!"

He handed me a backpack – leather.

"It has a blue-checkered pattern," he said. "There is a red and white strip across the pack that slopes up from left to right. The straps are black. Might be your thing."

The leather was amazing - supple, soft. I could almost hear the pack calling my name as I checked out the multiple pockets and imagined where I could put my computer, my phone, my clothes, and my toiletries. It was easily big enough to accommodate everything I might need on a weekend trip. Besides, it was an "LV." I would be the most stylish guy wherever I was.

This thing was perfect.

Then, I asked the price.

I tried not to gulp at the figure. I smiled at the salesperson, thanked her profusely, and said, "I'll think about it." I knew she'd heard that polite lie a thousand times.

We continued our journey up and down the Strip. We eventually stopped for a little blackjack. The dealers announce the cards for players who are blind. It was a great experience, especially since I won a couple of hundred!

When we finally got back to the hotel, we said goodnight and goodbye. My buddies had a 9 AM flight. My return flight left at 1:30 PM. I had the entire morning to myself - in Las Vegas.

I was still feeling down about the last competition. Following breakfast, I determined what I needed: retail therapy.

My mind went back to the Louis Vuitton store and to the Apollo backpack. I could still smell the leather.

Yep - time to go!

Nothing had changed in my life. I was still blind. How was I going to navigate the walk from the Flamingo to the Bellagio?

I had my cane, but I needed some navigation assistance.

I work with Aira a lot. It's a great company that utilizes technology to help visually-impaired individuals live more independently. Here's how it works.

Aira has agents available 24/7 with whom I can connect either through my phone or a pair of smart glasses. The agent can see my surroundings through the glasses or the camera on my phone and "talk me around" wherever I am.

"Lex, there's a mailbox to your left."

"Lex, the Cheerios are in front of you and up about two feet."

"Lex, what brand of paper towels do you prefer? Bounty's on the left – Brawny's one shelf down."

It all happens in real time – a phenomenal virtual door to the world.

I called Aira and got Connie. She was seated at her console, pulled me up on her screen, and said, "You have about a twenty-minute walk. Let's go."

Keep in mind, it can sometimes take me a little longer to get somewhere – especially in a new environment. What might be nine minutes for a sighted person may require a little more time for me.

I get down the elevator, which I could have handled on my own since the buttons are embossed with braille, and headed out into the sheering heat of a Nevada June. It was about half a click cooler than Hell.

The Boulevard was jammed with people. I could hear them. I could feel them. I could smell them. They were everywhere but I was ready for the challenge. No one ever got anywhere by standing still.

Sliding my cane back and forth, I weaved in and out of the mob. After decades of practice, the cane acts more like a sensor than a stick. I know when I touch a seam in the sidewalk or when I hit a loose pebble. Whenever I could, I stayed as close as possible to the curb. With the oncoming traffic to my right, I had a natural barrier and guide.

Connie kept me going in the right direction. "Cross street coming up, Lex."

"You have a big hotel on the left. There will be cars going in and out of the drive."

Finally, she said, "Okay, you have to cross the Boulevard on the skyway. We'll use the escalator."

There was an elevator – Connie pointed it out. But escalators are faster and I handle them very well – most of the time.

As you can imagine, since they are working off an image on a screen, Aira agents sometimes have restricted depth perception. In this case, I didn't have my smart glasses, so Connie was reading my situation from my cell phone camera – very limited contrast. Either she could not see both escalators (due to the way I was holding the phone) or she could not determine their direction. For whatever reason, I ended up trying to ascend the one that was going down.

After a while, I was pretty sure Connie had put me on a treadmill.

"I'm not getting anywhere," I said.

As soon as Connie recognized the situation, I am sure she was mortified. "Is there one to the right?"

I found it, stepped on, and crossed Las Vegas Boulevard without further incident. All the way across the skyway, however, I kept wondering how many people saw me trying to go the wrong way – and said nothing.

I'm not bitter. In hindsight, the situation was pretty funny.

But I still wonder.

After conquering the mystery of the wrong-way escalator, I kept moving towards the object of my quest. I crossed the Boulevard in good shape, took an *elevator* down to street level and kept moving. After a while, Connie said, "There it is!"

My heart rate increased. Louis Vuitton and the Apollo backpack were almost within reach. Except for one more, significant obstacle…

…a revolving door.

I knew it was there – I'd been through it just the day before. But I'd had help. Now, I had to maneuver it on my own.

Again, the people around me were scurrying this way and that. No one wanted to deal with getting me and my trusty cane through the whirling opening at one of the most luxurious hotels on the Strip.

I knew I would have to time it, so I stood and listened. The revolving cylinder made a noise, very subtle, but distinct – a dull, swishing slap – every time the door gaskets hit the frame. I started to count.

One…sh-rumph…two…sh-rumph…three…sh-rumph…four…*charge!*

I mis-timed my first step by a millisecond and was pinned. I wriggled into the cylinder, still in one piece despite my squishing, and dutifully followed the glass panel around in its little circle. When I felt the air-conditioned interior of the hotel, I stepped to my right – quickly. I was not going to be road-kill again.

I had made it. I could sense the elegance surrounding me.

Connie stayed with me even though the signal went in and out a little. There's a lot of stuff going on in Vegas and a lot of large structures that can obstruct cell signals. But we remained connected well enough for her to guide me to the door of nirvana – Louis Vuitton.

The voice greeting me was eager and refined. "May I help you, sir?"

"I'm interested in an Apollo backpack," I said. "The one that has the blue-checkered pattern with the red and white strip on the pack."

There was a slight pause. I think the clerk was a little thrown by the fact that I knew what color I wanted. Still, she offered me her elbow – Louis Vuitton employees are very-well trained – and guided me to a chair. Mr. Higgins would have been proud of her.

In less than a minute, I was caressing the soft leather and reexamining the satchel. Ah, this was the one.

"How much is it?" I asked. I already knew but I was hoping maybe there was a sale or something.

She told me.

There wasn't a sale. I knew I'd have to starve myself for a month, maybe two, but this baby was going home to California with me.

She swiped my card and put my purchase in a bag, then wished me well as I walked out of the store with my new leather Apollo. I was a very happy guy.

But the story wasn't over.

I checked the time. 12:30 PM. I had an hour. This was going to be close, but I had complete confidence in my ability to negotiate the trip to the airport.

I still had time. I pulled up my Uber app. Three minutes later, the app told me my ride was waiting.

All good – except I couldn't find it. I took the exit closest to the store. I could tell I was outside, but there wasn't any Uber. I thought I was standing on Las Vegas Boulevard but the more I investigated, the more I doubted my location.

About every ten feet, I came to a metal fence – circular. A few swipes of the cane told me there was a tree in the middle of every fence. I could hear traffic – sounded like the right place to me.

So, there I was, clutching a Louis Vuitton bag to my chest like a mother holding a newborn, knowing that any minute, someone could "relieve" me of my treasure.

I began to flag people down. Well, I tried. Most of them were laughing and talking. I could hear a few scurrying away. They must have thought I was begging or something.

My phone rang – the Uber driver. We talked for a while and tried to connect. I could not give him anything more than "I'm outside the Bellagio."

Eventually, he cancelled the ride.

I checked my phone. 12:56 PM.

Finally, a very cool gentleman – I never learned his name – escorted me around to the front.

"There is a designated area at all the hotels for rideshare pick-up," he explained as we walked. "Here we are. Good luck."

It was 1:06 when my ride came. He must have broken every traffic law in the book getting me to McCarran International. Still, by the time I got there, the woman at the counter informed me I was not going to make my flight.

There are a few things in life I detest. Missing flights stands very near the top of the list, just ahead of Brussel sprouts.

I wanted to go home.

I finally landed in San Diego about four hours later toting my fancy, Louis Vuitton Apollo backpack.

I think about my little adventure often. And when I do, I always say a special "thank you" to Mr. Higgins. He made my jaunt to the Bellagio possible by training me, working with me, and giving me the confidence to venture out on my own.

We all have limitations. The easy ones to overcome are physical. I can't see but I can still do lots of things.

The hardest limitations to conquer are the ones we set for ourselves in our own minds.

"I'd like to write a book, but no one would probably read it."

"I've always wanted to make furniture, but I might cut my hand."

"I thought about sending my song into the contest, but there's not chance it would win."

The list never ends.

I didn't want to use a cane because it set me apart - it made me different - and it wasn't very cool. But once I picked up my cane, once I silenced the voices in my head and heart, the world that had suddenly disappeared for me overflowed with opportunity and experiences.

If I'd never picked up my cane, I might be sitting in the dark someplace with a bag of chips and a beer, two hundred and eighty pounds of bitter, blind misery. But Mr. Higgins would not let that happen to me. The training was not always easy and it wasn't always fun.

I wanted to be a cane expert in the first three minutes.

It took time.

I got a little frustrated sometimes.

But I never gave up. Frankly, if I'd tried, my mother and Mr. Higgins would have "gently" changed my mind.

The longer I worked with the cane, the better I got.

And the world changed.

When we immerse ourselves in negativity or doubt, we embrace our limitations, limit our possibilities, and eliminate our opportunities. You may not have a cane but you have a pencil, a keyboard, a phone, a guitar – most importantly, you have a mind and a heart. Those are all pathways to success and happiness. They can alter your future and, perhaps, change lives along the way.

You might only touch one life – or, you could touch millions.

It's not always a bundle of laughs. It's never easy. But you *will* meet your destiny – you *will* help to shape the lives of those you love – if you do one, little thing.

Grab your cane – and go!

A Shot in the Dark

"Jamison with the board. Outlet to Cota. He crossed midcourt. Alley-oop to Carter *for the dunk!* And Carolina is beginning to impose its will!"

Woody Durham – voice of the Tar Heels for forty years. For almost as long as I can remember, I listened to him on the air as he vividly painted the action in both football and basketball. If you grow up in North Carolina and you love basketball, it's a requirement – like washing behind your ears, and going to church -- to learn about the game and pick a team.

The North Carolina State Wolfpack.

The Duke Blue Devils.

The Wake Forest Demon Deacons.

Or – drum roll, please…

… the University of North Carolina Tar Heels.

Is it even a contest? The Heels have produced some of the best players who ever laced 'em up. And the greatest player who ever set foot on the hardwood wore Carolina blue: His Airness – Michael Jordan. Of course, he was with the Chicago Bulls by the time I started paying attention to hoops, but everyone knew where his allegiance lay.

I can remember seeing some games on television before I lost my sight. After my world vanished, I became fascinated with the sounds of sports, especially basketball. The shouts of the crowd – the officials' whistles – rubber soles squeaking their way through hard-nosed defense – the deathly silence in the Dean Dome as one of the hometown heroes toes the line for a crucial free throw – and the deafening roar that threatened to overwhelm Woody's voice when a Tar Heel victory was assured.

I would still rather listen to any game on the radio. The announcers specialize in detail and telling images. Some people close their eyes and envision the court. I don't have to – I just listen and smile as an adept play-by-play "shows" me every nuance of the game.

I like to think I would have been a good basketball player. I stand between 6'1" and 6'2". I'm slender, pretty quick, and have long arms. Yep, I would have been good. I would have been a 3-point specialist. A sharp-shooter like Steph Curry.

While I could still see, I had a hard-plastic basketball hoop I got for Christmas one year. You put water in the base to keep it steady. I loved it but it eventually wore out and went to basketball hoop heaven. I never got a stand-alone hoop again.

I remember the day I got the Nerf net for my room. It hung on the closet door. I was so excited.

Ma wasn't wild about the ball because, given my more-than-occasional lack of accuracy, it left marks all over the wall. So, the ball disappeared and I was relegated to using socks – no kidding – three or four socks all wrapped together into a ball.

I could shoot it just fine – but it didn't dribble very well.

Problem was I never knew when I made or missed. Every kid thinks every shot is going in, but I knew even I would miss occasionally. So, I hit on the idea of closing the bottom of the net with a safety pin. When the socks - I mean, ball - went through successfully, the pin cradled it.

As you can imagine, it was challenging. I wasn't very good at the beginning. The ball didn't go in very much.

To get a feel, I stood directly in front of the net and dropped the ball into the hoop. I could hear it. Over and over and over. Then, from about a foot away. Over and over and over. Finally, I got to where I could make shots from everywhere.

My room was a decent size and I positioned my furniture to give me maximum "floor space."

After a while, I knew every shot from every position in my room. Mr. Higgins, my mom, and my grandmother had taught me the importance of memorizing landmarks. Once I practiced, I knew exactly how hard I needed to shoot from my dresser - Swish! From the bedroom door - Money! From the corner - bank shot off the board - Boom! And, from "downtown" across the room - Buckets!

I started getting fancier. I would throw the ball behind my back and shoot, fade away - swish! I would run (sort of given the limited space and, you know, the other thing), jump, and dunk it. I learned how to shoot a turnaround - Swish! I even perfected a move where I ran across the room, did a 180 and shot the ball with my back to the basket - Swish!

It was a fantastic feeling. Almost as soon as I let one fly, I knew if I had made it. The ball would go in. I would retrieve it and start my routine again and listen to Woody's voice in my head.

"Gillette has the ball on the baseline. Under 10 seconds left. Carolina down 1. He jab-steps right, goes left – 5 seconds. He crosses into the circle – 3...2. Gillette's in the air. He lets it fly from 16 feet. There's the buzzer. *It's good! It's good! Carolina wins by one on a sensational move by All-American Lex Gillette.*

**

That simple, little boy activity changed the trajectory of my life. The Nerf net was an actual goal – but it became somewhat of a symbol. We all need a goal, a target at which to aim, a mountain to climb, an object we need to stretch to touch, a time we need to beat, a book we need to write – we all need something.

I began to understand that if I could rig up a little Nerf net, if a blind kid in Raleigh could make a basketball shot, I could accomplish all sorts of things.

After I bought the net, I refused to take no for an answer. I'm no better than anyone else – I get distracted and discouraged. Those are natural reactions to life. Everyone fails. But what people remember is how you react to failure – what you do after you land on your butt because you missed the landing pit (more on that later).

Again, everyone fails. And anyone can quit. I could have abandoned my net the first time my mother said, "I better not see any more marks from that ball on my walls." But I took a sock, shoved it in another sock, shoved them into yet another sock, tied a tight knot in the end, cut off the excess, and made a "ball" I could use without getting into trouble.

Seems like a small thing, but it wasn't to me. I couldn't see the rim, but *I wanted to play basketball*.

The safety pin at the bottom of the net hardly rivals the invention of the microchip, but it revolutionized my approach to a simple game I played in my bedroom. A game I played for hours. A game that ultimately changed the world view I could see only in my head.

We live in an age where a lot of people do not want to spend the time to figure things out. They want the easy way – the quick answer – the expedient solution. I'm not going to get political or social here, but fewer and fewer people in society, government, and life seem willing to put in the effort to make things work. Time-saving devices are great but can anything substitute for the hours of enrichment we can get from reading *The Alchemist or Everybody, Always*? I've worked with Google before – an excellent company. But, would you rather have your kid ask Google a question about worms or go out, dig in the dirt, and find one to study up close?

We're creative beings capable of doing amazing things. We just have to put in the time. Do the work, be patient, anticipate the failures and meet the challenges. Set a goal, then pursue it with relentless perseverance.

You will grow.

You will ascend.

And, eventually, you will fly.

I still have the Nerf net. When I quit traveling so much, the very first thing I will move into my new house will be that little goal. It will occupy a permanent place of honor in my trophy room because my childhood basketball net reminds me of the importance of having a goal, and the challenges we all encounter when we have to take a shot in the dark.

After all, if you never take the shot, you will never score!

Find Your Wings

I can still see the green hose – an emerald, rubber garter snake running from the bib at the side of my grandmother's house, around the corner, and out into the backyard. Thing must have been over 100-feet long. Grandma didn't turn it on, the hose wasn't there for irrigation. It lay on the ground so I could use it.

Just like everyone else, I think my "Grandma" is the best. Despite a battle with Hodgkin's Lymphoma, she will probably pass her 78th birthday before this book is published.

I spent hours and hours at her home when I was a kid. And every time was a new adventure.

The hose was one of my first guides. It lay along the ground and let me know where I was in Grandma's expansive backyard. If I explored a little too far, I stepped carefully until I felt the reassuring curve of the hose under my foot. As long as I could locate the hose, I knew how to get back to the house.

Grandma's kitchen window overlooked the backyard. No matter what she was doing, I never left her sight. She was my ever-vigilant angel. We didn't know anything about "accessibility." No one ever breathed that word. In her own quiet way, Grandma created something others would "discover" decades later, all the while catapulting me to a higher level of independence.

Grandma: Remember when you were coming to tell me something and you dragged the hose with you? I asked you how you were going to go back out if you brought it with you.

Lex: Yes ma'am.

She is a wise woman, my grandmother. I never dragged the hose back in again.

One thing about being at Grandma's house, the rules did not change. Some kids go to see grandparents and come back spoiled and disrespectful. They get to run wild – do whatever they want. Not me. The expectations at my mother's house were the same as the ones she'd experienced as a child at my grandmother's. I toed the line in both places and everywhere in-between, and worked on being the very best version of myself that I could be. I used good manners, spoke respectfully to everyone, and did as I was instructed without any "back talk."

The consistency brought comfort. I knew what to do and how to do it. Life might have been regimented, but it was far from rigid.

Man, I could have some fun at Grandma's.

Lex: Ain't no more ponds back there now – no ponds to go fishing.

Grandma: We can make one right now. It won't take us long. Just say the word. We sure can make one – say the word.

"Ponds" is a little grandiose. My grandmother's backyard had several significant depressions. They weren't holes, just extended low areas where water gathered after a typical, southern gully-washer. Once the weather cleared - Grandma would not allow me to cavort in the lightning – we turned our imaginations loose on those little bodies of water.

They became grand oceans across which we would voyage to far-off lands – treacherous swamps we explored (while keeping a wary eye out for gators and such). Grandma had a pair of rubber boots that I always wore on our adventures. Never mind that they almost came up to my thighs, I was fearless and intrepid.

We "fished" those ponds, sometimes while holding sticks and others while casting make believe lines from invisible rods. We caught all sorts of things: bass and crappie, trout and salmon, sometimes sharks and barracuda.

The fish routinely put up a mighty struggle but with tenacity, skill, and strength (particularly on my part – I liked to see myself as a strongman), we always prevailed. We displayed our prizes to one another with great pride, comparing who brought in the larger trophy.

Sometimes I went "swimming." Even though there was not enough room for two full strokes, I thrashed around like a brown-skinned Michael Phelps, hauling in medals or saving someone who was in distress. Grandma played right along, her luminescent mind fueling my ever-widening imagination.

Grandma lives in La Grange, North Carolina, a wide spot some forty-seven miles "up the road" from Greenville. The little town of about 2800 souls is most notable as the home of The Corsairs (a doo-wop group of the early 60s') and Frank Lucas, the infamous drug kingpin who was portrayed by Denzel Washington in *American Gangster*. It is a quiet place where it's nearly impossible to go more than fifty yards without running into someone who knows you – or, in my case, who recognizes you as Mary's little grandson."

I loved my summer days there. More than anything, though, I loved the journeys I took with Grandma.

Grandma: There you go...I know you didn't want to watch TV all day. You were always into something. You loved to say, "Let's think of something we can do."

Lex: We went lots of places – other countries and such.

Grandma: Yes, we did – what's the word? (I think she was looking for "virtual.") But we went before we were able to get there. Yes indeed. We could do everything but talk their language. But I bet if we practiced, we could've – yes, indeed.

I cannot think of too many places Grandma and I did not visit in our imaginary adventures. France, Spain, Russia (it was still a very scary place to go back then)... the Arctic. We would "fly" there, then explore the new place. We met interesting people and interacted with unfamiliar cultures. We played different roles.

And, in my mind, I could see it all.

Although I had no way of knowing at the time, "traveling" with Grandma provided invaluable practice for me. When the time came for the real thing, I wasn't nearly as afraid as I might otherwise have been.

Lex: I used to throw the ball up on the house. Remember?

Grandma: Uh-huh. You remember, sometimes I'd jump in front of you and catch it and you'd still be there waiting on it to come down.

Lex: Yes, ma'am.

Grandma (unleashing her trademark Grandma chuckle): Yes, we had a good time.

I invented a game to pass the time – but it was more than something to deflect boredom. I wanted to push myself – to discover what I could master even though I could not see.

The back of Grandma's house, just over the back porch, sloped at about a 45°angle. I liked to heave an old soccer ball up on the roof. I'd listen as it bounced, settled, and began to roll. I learned to "read" where it was going to come off the roof.

If I caught the ball in the air, I gave myself two points. If I caught it on the bounce, I got one. Sometimes it smacked me in the nose. Sometimes, it got away and I had to search for it a while. And, as she mentioned, sometimes, "someone's" sneaky granny would slide up from the side and take it before it got to me.

I spent hours throwing, tracking, and catching that ball.

I wonder if it's still at Grandma's house.

Not all my playtime was alone.

Grandma: When your cousins came over, you did a lot of things. You used to swing on that chain.

Lex: Is that chain still on the tree?

Grandma: It surely is. You were the very last one to swing on it – to swing on that chain.

Lex: How old is that tree?

Grandma: Lord, I don't know. It was here when I got here.

Lex: It's still big and strong.

Grandma: Yes, it is - way up in the air.

The tree still dominates the yard to the left of my grandmother's house. In truth, I'm not sure what it is. I suspect it's an oak - because of age and size. My arms are long - I have a reach of almost seven feet. I can't come close to wrapping my arms around the tree. It would take two of me to hug that old boy.

Gnarled roots jab out of the ground. The upper branches pierce the sky. An old chain hangs from one of the branches. There's a knot in the chain about five feet off the ground.

We took turns. Swinging on that chain was a blast. With each pass, I swung higher and higher. When my feet hit the tree, I'd plant them against the trunk and push.

Some days, I was an adventurer saving the world. Sometimes I was Tarzan, leading the animals on a charge through the jungle. The tree and that old chain fueled the games I played in my head. When I was swinging from that branch, I had no limitations. My child's game became a symbol of who I would become - a man who recognizes no barriers.

Grandma's house provided me with hour upon hour of fun and adventure. But it wasn't the only place I visited when I was in La Grange.

Grandma: I used to watch you walk down to Cousin Liddy's store. You remember. I stood on the porch and made sure you got there.

Lex: Going to get them cookies. I liked that. She used to throw some extra in there, too.

Grandma: I watched you going down and she made sure you got back. Watched you all the way into the yard. Yes, indeed.

Lex: I remember how the road felt right in front.

Grandma: That big dip right before you got to the door. You'd go down in that dip, then right up the steps. She had everything a kid could want. Right after the big dip in the walkway, I'd mount the steps – three if I recall correctly – and walk in the store past the screen door, an old, creaky thing. The floor was linoleum tile over wood. I remember the very distinctive sound my shoes made when I walked around the store.

Cousin Liddy had a metal rack stuffed with all the chips and the like. They hung from a hole in the top middle of the package – Bugles, Fritos, Hot Fries – everything.

Cousin Liddy sold Butter Cookies, the little round ones shaped like a flower with a hole in the center. Oh, they went down smooth. I liked to buy those. And ginger snaps – those crisp little cookies that tasted like gingerbread and Christmas all rolled into one.

I'm sure Cousin Liddy gave me more cookies than I purchased. That was okay with me.

In North Carolina at the time, at least in my part of the world, the drink of choice was Pepsi Cola. It originated in New Bern, NC just fifty miles west on Highway 70. Cousin Liddy kept the drinks in an old-style drink box. You used to see a lot of them in "country stores." Usually decorated with a company logo, the refrigerated boxes looked like chest-style freezers. And they kept drinks colder than cold. I had to sort of slide my shoulder into the box to get a drink from as close to the bottom as possible and scramble back to my feet. I paid for the soda and took it back home where Grandma had the bottle-opener ready.

Oh, I can still hear the sound of the *hiss* as Grandma popped the top and the rattle of the cap as it hit the kitchen floor. Nothing has ever tasted better to me than that first sip of an ice-cold Pepsi on a sticky July day in North Carolina. The beverage was so cold, it burned all the way down – burned and soothed all at the same time.

I was a happy, happy boy.

Two toys stand out from my days at Grandma's. The first was a black, 18-wheel truck complete with cab and trailer. It had a crank on the side. When I turned it, the truck growled to life. Pressing on the top produced the distinctive *waaaah, waaaah* we've all heard on the interstate. The lights on the front worked, too. It was a really cool truck.

I bet I put 200,000 miles on that thing. The doors on the back of the trailer opened. I delivered crates of Pepsi to Seattle and cars to Mississippi. I transported fur coats to Minnesota (even though I wasn't sure where it was for a while) and cowboy hats to Dallas (what else would they need, right). Every load involved a new destination and a new adventure. And Grandma was along for most every cross-country trek.

Last time I was at Grandma's, she brought my old, reliable rig out of the closet. She keeps it there – just in case I need to haul a little freight.

Lex: I remember the little green thing I swung in the air – made a screeching noise.

Grandma: Yes, indeed. Woo – woo – woo.

The details are a little fuzzy, but I had a tubular toy about three-feet long and two-inches around. It had some flex to it, and when I swung it, it made a *skreeeeee* sound. The faster it went, the higher the pitch. I loved it.

Thinking back, I'm surprised Grandma didn't burn it.

Whether I was there during the summer or at a holiday, my grandmother could throw down in the kitchen. She cooked like she invented it. Breakfasts were astounding – grits, sausage, eggs, toast – everything I ever wanted. And on Thanksgiving Day, Grandma brought her "A" game. There was every imaginable dish on the table and no one went away hungry – if they could stand up to move away from the table. When it was time to "chow down," my grandmother could out-cook anyone on the planet.

I spent a lot of hours taste-testing her food. It was tough work, but someone had to do it. Ha!

I owe a lot to my grandmother. She loves me to this very day – and I am devoted to her. But the greatest gift she gave me was the freedom of my mind.

Grandma: You could imagine in your mind what things looked like and you could remember when you had your sight and put two and two together. What can you not do now that you would like to do? Did I say that right?

Lex: Yes, ma'am, you did. (I did not have an answer. There's nothing.)

Grandma: Remember how I would ask you, "Elexis, why do you pace around like that?" And you would say, "I'm thinking."

Lex: Yes, ma'am.

Grandma: Well, you're still thinking, aren't you?

Lex: Yes, ma'am. I'm still thinking.

A little house with a huge tree and a garden hose out back served as my trampoline into creativity. I learned there is more to sight than seeing and that true adventure takes place in the mind.

In many ways, my grandmother is like any other. She is a security blanket, a source of safety and comfort. She stands as a light in any darkness and a wall against any danger. She is fierce in her devotion, dedicated in her teaching, demanding in her quest for excellence, and overwhelming in her affection.

But she is special because she is *my* grandma. She was present as my glimpses of this world grew indistinct, then faded to black. She could not do anything about my sightlessness, but she was not going to let me be blind to the endless possibilities of life.

She cultivated a garden of hope in my young heart and held before me a magical window through which I could envision the future. Playful and imaginative, she birthed dreams just as surely as she'd brought my mother into the world. She set me up to conquer every challenge I ever encountered.

Somehow, with her tender concern, simple ways, and earthy wisdom, she convinced a frightened youngster who had lost his sight that he could – should – and eventually would – fly.

God bless you, Grandma. I love you.

And thank you for the wings.

See More, Be More

"Straight! Straight! Straight!"

Coach Whitmer's voice cut through the air like a hot knife through butter. "Straight! Straight! Straight!"

I could hear his hands clapping as I ran straight toward the sound. I took a couple of strides forward, then leapt into the abyss. Soft sand greeted me.

"Good job," Coach Whitmer said.

That wasn't exactly what I was thinking. This was some weird stuff.

Coach was still talking. "Just focus. Keep following the sound of my voice. There's nothing around you," he said. "Take five strides and then jump straight ahead. You gotta trust me on this."

That was easy for him to say. He could see where he was going.

He lined me up on the runway once again. I heard him walk away toward the takeoff board. "Okay," he said. "Straight! Straight! Straight!"

I ran to the sound of his voice and jumped again. This time the sand felt like a warm handshake. I was starting to like it.

"Niiice," he said.

I bet you're probably wondering how I got started in all this. Well, it began in gym class one day at Athens Drive High School in Raleigh, North Carolina.

**

Navigating the halls of a large high school wasn't as hard as you might suspect. I had the power in my hands, my white cane. When I walked down the halls, sliding my cane from right to left, kids cleared a walking lane like the Red Sea getting out of Moses' way. No one wanted to get hit, and even though kids can be mean, no one wanted to be responsible for tripping "the blind kid" or to have their legs unintentionally whip-sawed from beneath them by my daredevil cane.

After losing my sight, I could've easily attended a school dedicated to servicing the visually impaired. After all, the Governor Morehead School, the eighth school for the blind established in the United States, is in Raleigh. But my mom made the decision to keep me in public school because she felt it would benefit me more in the long-run to have constant interaction with sighted peers.

To thrive in a public-school setting, I was granted certain accommodations. I needed my textbooks in braille and I had a braille writer. It was similar to an old-school typewriter, but it only had nine buttons. Sounds weird, I know, but braille is a lot different from print. On a standard QWERTY keyboard, you press your left pinky for the letter A or your right pointer finger for the letter J. Since you use a computer every day, you probably type without thinking about it.

Braille writers are not laid out the same. The letters are formed by a combination of raised dots. Take the letter A. In braille, it's only one dot, so you press one key. The letter J consists of three dots, so you have to press three keys simultaneously. The difficult thing is knowing which ones to press. The letters D, F, H, J, L, M, O, S, and

U are all made up of three dots, but each one is formed by pressing a different combination of three keys. You differentiate the letters by the positioning of the three dots. And you thought high-school French was hard.

It took me a year to learn the entire braille code, but knowing the alphabet enabled me to advance through school. All of my textbooks were in braille, which sounds nice until you understand that each 8.5/11" sheet of paper equals about two pages in braille. Sometimes a standard book written in English requires multiple braille volumes. The *Book of Genesis* for me is about the size of an old phone book. The entire Bible takes about eighteen volumes of the same size. That was loads of fun on Sunday mornings. I felt like I needed one of those flatbed carts from Sam's Club to get the book into the sanctuary.

I made one significant adjustment in high school. "Elexis" morphed into "Lex." First, a lot of the teachers butchered my name: "Alex," "Alexis," "Eeee-lexsis," some I cannot even remember. Second, at the beginning of the first year, when no one knew me, a lot of people were surprised to hear a male voice respond "Here" when the teacher called what seemed to be a female name. So, I went with Lex at school. At home, with old friends, and forever in my heart, I am "Elexis."

While attending Athens Drive High School, I met someone who changed my life – Mr. Brian Whitmer. He headed up the Visually Impaired Program at our school. The VIP dedicated itself to assisting children with vision-related issues and helping us to succeed in a public-school classroom setting.

Mr. Whitmer ordered the textbooks we needed. On the first day of the school year, my books were waiting. I always asked my teachers in advance which pages we would be covering. I wanted to avoid carrying multiple volumes to class each day. It was tough-going, but, as the saying goes, "You gotta do what you gotta do."

I completed my class assignments and homework on a braille writer. Each VIP had braillists, individuals trained in reading and writing braille. When I turned in my work, the braillists transcribed my "dots" into print, so the teachers could grade it.

Early on I learned that Mr. Whitmer did not play. He had the same mindset as my mom. You go to school to learn – that's a student's only job. If you're not learning, then what are you doing? You better believe I did everything in my power to stay on-task. It wouldn't be good for Mr. Whitmer to issue a report to my mom stating that I wasn't doing my job. She was the boss and, let me tell you, not one you wanted to be angry.

But Mr. Whitmer was cool, too. He attended P.E. class with me. He always made sure I was in an inclusive environment, one where I could be involved in all of the games alongside my classmates. And he was instrumental in what turned out to be a pivotal day in my life.

**

I dropped my bag on the locker-room bench and yelled. "Hey, how 'bout them Tar Heels!"

A few feet to my left, someone responded, "Be quiet."

I've never been shy about my love of the University of North Carolina. Like I said, when you live in Raleigh, a corner of the Research Triangle, you have to like either UNC, N.C. State, or that other blue school. I figured I'd found a "non-believer." I began getting dressed for P.E. Class. "What are we doing today?" I asked figuring someone would answer.

The same voice said, "We're testing."

Ah. I remembered. All of the students in our high school had to participate in a nationwide physical fitness test that measured our ability in certain exercises like pushups, pullups, and sit-ups. I swapped out my jeans and tee-shirt for a pair of basketball shorts and a tank top. I was ready to go! Since I come from an athletic family, I was eager to test out my skills. I had to do well for my family's name.

Coach Scott called the roll "Jones."

"Here!"

"Michaels."

"Present."

And on down the list. We split into groups – different bunches of boys and girls for each station. An instructor gave directions, explaining how we were measured, keeping track of the time, and recording the results. Once each group completed a particular exercise, Coach Scott blew the whistle and we went to the next event. Mr. Whitmer accompanied me from station to station.

"Are you ready Lex?" he asked.

"I was born ready," I said with the certain confidence of a young teen.

We began with sit-ups. Oh man, I started cranking them out. One, two, three, four, five, six. I was firing on all cylinders. I could hear Whitmer's voice from above. "Come on Lex, keep going!"

After a while, my abs started to burn, but I did not stop. No one had called "Time." Fatigue started to tickle at my abs with a burning finger. My reps got a little slower. But I pushed for another one – then another.

Finally, someone mercifully said, "And... stop!"

Thank God.

I staggered to my feet. Mr. Whitmer guided me to the side of the gym where I put my back against the wall and slid down into a seated position. Huffing and puffing from the other participating students filled the air. This was serious business. It was all about bragging rights – locker banter – man stuff!

A shrill whistle echoed around the gym and we moved to the next station: the standing long-jump. You stood just behind a line, pumped your arms back and forth, and then jumped as far as you could. You had to leave from both feet – no running – no "wind-up" step. Each student got two attempts. A measuring tape stretched across the floor immediately showed everyone how far each student jumped. I could track the event by the sounds.

"Abernathy, you're up."

Grunt.

Thump.

"Six feet, ten inches."

Then – "Gillette."

Mr. Whitmer positioned me behind the starting point. I bent my knees, put my arms back, and hurled myself forward. It didn't seem like I was in the air long at all. My feet hit the ground. I absorbed the shock by bending my knees, then I stood up.

Off to the side, I heard voices. Some of my classmates were giggling. What was so funny?

Mr. Whitmer helped me out of the way and to the back of the line where we waited for my second attempt. Mr. Whitmer laughed out loud, a hearty laugh full of excitement.

"Lex that was good – like really good!"

I smiled. "How far did I go?"

"Nine feet and eight inches," he responded.

I'd heard all the results. Most of my classmates were going somewhere between seven and eight feet. A few of the guys cleared nine feet, but not too many.

I could feel the competitive juices kick in – I needed to surpass my previous mark. I had to go farther. I listened to each pair of feet land.

"Lex, you're up."

Once again, Mr. Whitmer placed his hand on my shoulder and led me to the starting point.

Focus, Lex, I thought.

I bent my knees slowly and let my arms hang as loosely as possible. Then, I exploded into the air. I tried to fly as long as possible but my feet finally touched down.

My first thought was, *Dang, I could've gone farther than that!*

I could hear the murmuring but I didn't hear a number. Both my jumps felt the same.

Somebody give me a result – I want a number!

Mr. Whitmer was laughing again. "Lex you went ten feet," he said. "You have one of the top marks in the entire school!"

Oh man, I felt fantastic. We had over 1500 students at Athens and I had one of the top marks in the entire school as a freshman. I walked on air the rest of the day, but I don't know who was more excited – me or Mr. Whitmer.

A little later in the day, he said, "Lex do you know what this means?"

"No. Not exactly," I said. "I guess it means I'm better at something than someone who can see?"

"Well, yes," he said, "but this is huge. You could possibly compete in the Paralympic Games one day."

"The what?" I asked.

"The Paralympic Games. It's an elite level competition for athletes who have a physical disability."

Everyone knew about the Olympic Games. Heck, I knew about Donovan Bailey, Michael Johnson, and Carl Lewis. And everyone in North Carolina knew about Marion Jones. She played basketball and ran track for the Tar Heels and trained in Raleigh. But I'd never heard of this other thing – the Paralympic Games.

Mr. Whitmer was almost babbling with excitement. "You could potentially be a track and field star. They have so many events that you can participate in, and one is the long-jump."

He continued, "You could represent the United States of America in competition, travel the world, and win medals."

Sounded pretty good to me – well, the medals part did. I wasn't so keen on the travel business. I figured it involved airplanes and the thought of flying frightened me a little.

But I am very competitive.

"So, would it work like P.E. class?" I asked. "Just line up and jump?"

I figured if I'd beaten almost everyone at my school, I'd probably have a good chance of beating some other kids from other places – especially when I got a little older – and practiced some. Besides, all the kids so far could see and I beat them. I should crush someone who was visually-impaired. Mr. Whitmer hesitated a little.

Uh oh.

"Ah, not exactly," he said. "What you just did was the standing long-jump. The one in which you would compete involves some running."

"How much running?" I asked. This was beginning to sound a tad more complicated than the Presidential Physical Fitness Test.

"Well, you run down a track – a little more than a hundred feet. Then, you jump and land in a big pile of sand."

I'd heard about "reading the fine print before." I was beginning to understand what it meant.

My first thought was, "Are you nuts?" But my mom taught me to be respectful to everyone, even crazy people. Mr. Whitmer replied. "You have to run first and then jump. You'll land in a big sand pit."

See, this is why you're always encouraged to read the fine print. Here came the questions:

I have to do what?

Run how far?

Jump from where?

How do I know if I'm running in the right direction, much less straight?

If I get hurt, will my mom's insurance cover it?

"Mr. Whitmer," I said. "I don't get it."

"Completely understandable," he said. "After you practice for a long time, you'll get really good. It'll all seem very natural. I'll line you up at the beginning. When I say "Go," you run toward the sound of my voice. Once you get to the takeoff spot, you jump as far as you can."

"How do I know how many steps to take?" I asked.

"We'll count them out – I promise we'll work everything out on the track. How about we go to the track and we'll walk through everything. You'll be great."

Now I know I'm dealing with someone who has lost it. But I just nodded.

"Great," Mr. Whitmer said. "We'll walk out there tomorrow."

I was saved when the final bell of the day rang, but for the rest of the day, I thought about what Mr. Whitmer wanted me to do. And I thought about everything he'd told all through class the next day – representing my country, traveling the world, competing in the Para-something I'd never heard of before. Strange. The longer I turned things over in my mind, the more I began to believe. I had no idea what was involved but by the end of the day, I was fired up and ready to go to the Paralympics.

As soon as the bell clanged, I jetted out of class and made my way to the opposite side of school where the locker room and gym were located. It was time for P.E. Class and I was more than a little eager to find out more about this long-jumping business.

Mr. Whitmer met me inside the gym. "You up for going down to the track today, Lex?"

"Yes, let's make it happen," I said.

The second we stepped outside, the muggy Carolina air jumped on us like a wet Labrador Retriever. We sweated our way to the track. Mr. Whitmer led me over to one end where he walked me along the long-jump runway.

"This is it," he said.

Feedback from my trusty cane told me this thing was not very wide – about three feet. Very little room for veering. I would have to run straight as a string. Not wide, but long – very long.

We walked to the other end.

"We're coming up on the sand pit," Mr. Whitmer said.

My cane tapped something wooden. I reached down and felt a board.

"That's the takeoff board," Mr. Whitmer said. It was a small, wooden board positioned in the ground. Mr. Whitmer continued. "In the Paralympics, they use a one-meter take-off zone."

A few taps later, my cane hit something soft – the sand pit.

"So," Mr. Whitmer said. His voice was a little high-pitched. He sounded very excited. "You will run as fast as you can, then leap forward into the sand. The officials sprinkle powder on the take-off zone and measure the distance from the front of your leading footprint to the first mark you make in the sand to determine how far you went."

I was examining the pit. End-to-end, side-to-side. It seemed pretty big – pretty hard to miss.

At least for the guys who could see it.

Still, I didn't imagine anyone was going to jump over it. That seemed like a good safety feature.

The explanation continued. "What I'm going to do is stand in between the takeoff board and the sand pit, clap my hands and yell, 'Straight!' You'll run directly to the sound of my voice. You'll have to mark off your steps."

"What does that mean?" I asked.

Mr. Whitmer guided me to the board. "You are facing the pit," he said. Then, he turned me around. "Now, your back is to the pit."

I nodded.

"Take five huge steps straight ahead."

I followed the instructions. One... two... three... four ... five.

Mr. Whitmer's voice drew closer. "I'm putting a cone right next to you, so we'll know where you started."

More nodding from me. I could feel my throat getting tight but I also felt the oddest sense of excitement.

"Let's review," he said. "How many steps did you take?"

"Five."

"Okay," he said. "I'm going to point you back toward the pit. When I say go, come right to the sound of my voice. Five big steps, then jump. Got it?"

"Got it."

Five steps this way – five steps that way. At least the math made sense.

"You ready to try it out?"

I nodded.

Mr. Whitmer's voice was calm and confident. "Lex, we're not going for any records here. This is not a competition. You're just trying it out to see if you like it. okay?"

Again, I nodded.

"All right. Hang on."

I heard his footsteps going away. When he called to me, I could tell he was farther away, but it was also obvious to me that he was directly in front of me. "You ready?" he asked.

I wasn't. But I nodded again out of habit.

"Come toward my voice, count five strides and take a little jump. You'll be fine," he said. "Ready? Go."

I started to jog. Mr. Whitmer's voice hit me right in the face. "Straight! Straight! Straight!" He was shouting and clapping at the same time.

I counted, one...two...three...four...five, gulped and took a half-hearted jump. I hit the sand standing up.

If I've ever been more frightened in my life, I don't remember it. Running – at any speed – and hurling yourself towards something you cannot see is unimaginably nerve-wracking.

I had no idea if I was going to hit the sand or the side of a Buick. It was, in every sense of the phrase, "a leap of faith."

Faith in Mr. Whitmer.

And faith in myself.

"Awesome!" Mr. Whitmer said. "How did it feel?"

"Like a decayed tooth," I responded.

He laughed at my response. "Well you did great for a first try. It's going to feel strange for a while. You'll have to work at it to get any good."

Here's the truth. I was completely out of my depth. Nothing was remotely close to my comfort zone. In the gym, I'd been still, then I jumped. I'd heard others do it. No one had so much as tweaked an ankle. It was fun. It was safe. I was good at it.

This was something entirely different. This business required another human being to navigate me from Point A to Point B while I was supposed to be moving at top speed. I simply did not have it in me to trust another person that much.

I didn't know any of my surroundings. I liked Mr. Whitmer and all, but he wasn't my mom. He'd always been nice to me but – geez…

I wondered if Mr. Whitmer had hit his head or something. This was the craziest idea I'd ever heard. All I did was jump from one spot on the gym floor to another one and all of a sudden, he has me traveling all over the world and winning medals because I am going to be nuts enough to race along a sidewalk and jump into a sand box surrounded by concrete.

"You sure about this, Mr. Whitmer?" I asked. "Seems to me like a lot of things could go wrong."

His arm rested on my shoulder. "It's going to feel uncomfortable. It's going to be challenging, but you can rest assured of this. I'll be your eyes. I'm not going to allow you to get hurt. You're not going to run into anything. You'll be safe. I will never let you down."

I could hear the conviction in his voice. "You're right," he said. "So many things could go wrong. On the other hand, so many things could go right. And when they do – it'll be great!"

I always appreciated how Mr. Whitmer challenged me, challenged my thinking, challenged my ability. Even though I still had misgivings, I had to admit that he was spot on. Sure, so many things could go wrong, and I could keep holding on to those thoughts as if I were holding for dear life to the edge of a cliff.

But what might happen if I let myself go? What might life look like if I threw myself into a quest like this? The thoughts were overwhelming and – at the time – completely unrealistic. I'm not sure I'd ever watched an Olympic Games, but I'd definitely never seen the long-jump.

Could I compete in something I'd never witnessed with my own eyes? But I was willing to try. I saw myself in a foreign country wearing a jersey with USA splayed across the front. I imagined bending over for a woman to drape a gold medal around my neck. The crowd would only stop cheering long enough to sing *The Star-Spangled Banner* and I would have the biggest of all smiles as I sang, "And the home of the brave!"

Mr. Whitmer interrupted my daydream. "Let's try again," he said.

"Straight! Straight! Straight!"

...four...five...this time I give the jump more effort. I let go of the controls a little – sort of threw myself at the end of the pit. After I landed, my stomach we still a little tight – I was still a little nervous. But I started to feel something else.

A magnetic sensation crept through my body. Without thinking, I walked over to Mr. Whitmer and said, "Again."

I kept lining up – and I kept jumping. I could not shake the images in my head. I could not rid my body of the increasing thrill of flight. While gravity, that immutable law of physics, was trying to keep me on the ground, the vision in my head and heart of what *might* happen was yanking me up into the clouds.

It was a tug-of-war.

And gravity was losing.

Every time I jumped, another boundary fell. Every time I hit the sand, I wiped out another border. Every time I followed the "Straight! Straight! Straight!" of Mr. Whitmer's voice, I shattered another restriction.

Funny thing about vision. No two people see the same object (or opportunity) the same way. To one person, a set of track and field spikes looks like a funny pair of shoes. To someone else, they look an awful lot like the opportunity for a free college education. Still another individual imagines that set of footwear will run all the way to the Paralympic Games.

Mr. Whitmer fixed his gaze on making me an athlete. His daily encouragement and constant motivation welded me to his vision.

That thing – that feat – that event – that opportunity in the future represents a treasure of sorts. It's a "pot of gold" in terms of life and happiness, and it's meant for you and everyone in your life. When something good happens to you, it lifts everyone with whom you are associated.

One man refused to allow me to remain in a state of blindness. One man did for me what we can all do for someone else. We can help others "see" more, so they can eventually "be" more.

Remove the Blindfold

One of the first things people ask me when they watch a Paralympic long-jump competition is, "Why are you wearing a blindfold?"

It's a logical inquiry and there is a logical answer.

An individual can be "legally" blind while still having some sight. Others, like me, cannot see the proverbial hand in front of our faces. To ensure a level playing field, all long-jump competitors in my division must wear a blindfold. While there is no set design, the blindfolds are all examined to guarantee they conform with the International Paralympic Committee Standards.

Let's expand my explanation a bit. There are three categories of visual impairment in the Paralympics: 11, 12, and 13. Without getting too technical, here are the distinctions. T11/F11 athletes have very little visual acuity and/or no light perception. The next level, T12/F12 competitors, while having higher visual acuity, have a visual field of less than 5° radius. The last category, T13/F13 encompasses athletes with the least severe visual impairment – but they still have a visual field of less than 20° radius. I am in the T11 category; a blindfold is mandatory.

When you compete as an 11, you must use a guide. Makes sense – we have a blindfold – someone needs to tell us where to go. You don't want athletes colliding at full speed.

In the lead-up to the 2016 Rio Games, I was fortunate enough to be sponsored by Nike. They supplied me with countless amounts of shoes and training apparel to ensure my success on the field of play.

The good folks at Nike decided they would design a special blindfold for me. It was a fascinating process – totally cool – and a lot of fun. They designed a "cooling hood" for Ashton Eaton and a hijab for female, Muslim athletes.

In today's track and field competitions, every millisecond counts – every centimeter is important. Every piece of gear from shoes to swimsuits undergoes rigorous test to reveal the slightest bit of excess weight or drag. Making an athlete a quarter-step quicker – helping a jumper stretch one centimeter farther – can mean the difference between standing atop the podium or watching the awards ceremony from the tunnel.

Michael Sarantakos from Nike began discussions about designing a performance blindfold for me – there's an oxymoron: *performance blindfold!* We worked on the project together with Baron Brandt, an inventor who spent a lot of time with measurements, 3D images, and prototypes.

One of the first things I told them about the blindfold was that I needed to be able to open my eyes. I couldn't have something smashing my eyelashes every time I blinked. Whatever material they used had to be breathable. I didn't want to feel like I'd stuck my head in a plastic sack.

And – here is perhaps the most important part – it needed to look really cool. After more than a few discussions, they figured out I wanted something with a Dark Knight feel. (Yes, my favorite superhero.)

Using notes from our conversations, the Design Team started in on the sketches. Baron used an amazing 3D program called "Blender" for the mock-up. Over the next month, he sent me three rounds of samples. We were on the clock because everyone wanted the new blindfold by the Rio Games. This was something I needed to have in advance. I had to train with it. I couldn't just walk out at the Paralympic Games and have someone strap something around my head: "Here, try this!"

What Baron designed was light, breathable, drag-free, and absolutely sick! The blindfold was a beautiful blue – went great with my uniform.

He even designed a special metal box to hold it, engraved with my motto in braille: "No need for sight when you have a vision."

The icing on the cake was when Michael and Baron flew down from Portland to San Diego to present me with my new performance blindfold. There was one more surprise the two of them had kept from me. When Michael handed me the blindfold, he asked, "Notice anything?"

My fingers ran along the edges of my new superhero mask. Stamped on the inside left (in braille) were the words, "No Fear." A huge, Kool-Aid smile split my face. The text constantly reminds me that when it's time to take on the world in competition, anxiety has no place – courage and confidence rule!

I had a blast working with the Nike crew.

Many of my sponsors have come to visit the Chula Vista Elite Athlete Training Center. It's a 155-acre, high-performance facility dedicated to helping athletes achieve peak levels. There's a track (I spend a lot of time here every day), a weight room for me to get buff, the sports medicine building, three BMX tracks, a state-of-the-art archery complex, a number of fields used for soccer, rugby, field hockey and lacrosse, and last but not least, the cafeteria (where I can regularly be found as well).

The CVEATC is a phenomenal facility and I enjoy showing it off to sponsors and other visitors. One question I get a lot is, "Lex, are you going to get into coaching once you're done competing?"

I have no interest in being an athletics coach, but over the years I've gotten into another form of coaching – leading experiential learning programs for companies. Senior-level employees of corporations like Facebook, Walmart, and BP have enjoyed participating in a program I facilitate called "The Guide Running Experience."

It's one thing to watch an athlete run while wearing a blindfold, but it's quite something different when you do it yourself. In the program, participants get the chance to run on the track where I train and to assume the role of an athlete or a guide.

Guess what? If you're "the athlete," you get the honor of wearing a blindfold, but don't worry, your guide or colleague, will be running directly beside you, ensuring that you make it safely from the starting mark to the finish line. I'm not sure I've ever seen anything that I could remotely label as "a sprint," but all of the participants are game and give it their best. Many of you may have experienced a "trust walk" where someone leads you around. Imagine doing that as fast as you can move.

Think that sounds scary? Well, it's nothing compared to giving the long jump a try – blindfolded.

As I am preparing for a jump, my guide lines me up and then jogs to the pit area. When it's "Go Time," I run towards the sound of his voice as fast as I can. I run with the confidence that my guide will move out of the way at the last possible second. I've got my approach down pat, so on the sixteenth step, I plant, fly through the air, and land in the sand.

No one stands next to you during your long-jump approach. You put on the blindfold, charge down the runway, all the while focusing on the voice calling to you: "Go, go, go, go!" Then, you launch yourself into the air and travel as far as you can. For safety reasons, I never ask my participants to jump. I just want them to feel what it's like to run alone, sightless, led only by a colleague's voice. It's a totally different feel from running next to someone who helps you make small adjustments and who makes sure you are running in a straight line.

Sometimes participants are a little hesitant and rightfully so. I remember my own reluctance. And the folks in my program did not rise to their levels of responsibility by taking foolish chances – they are smart and calculated. But, every last one of them is game. They make a good effort.

Recently, I facilitated The Guide Running Experience for a number of senior-level employees from Facebook. During the debrief, one of the gentlemen said, "You know what? I've climbed mountains, I've been skydiving, but wearing a blindfold and running is by far the hardest thing I've ever done."

Wow! That blew my mind. I've been skydiving. (Somehow you knew that, didn't you?) You go through the training session, scramble into the plane, take off, and climb to between 10,000 and 13,000 feet. When the doors opened, all I could feel was the rush of the wind – all I could hear was the engine whining. I knew the only way to get to the ground was out of the open door. Of course, every first jump is in tandem, but I am very accustomed to working with a teammate, so out of the door we went.

Then I started thinking about all the things that could go wrong.

The comment about, "Wearing a blindfold and running is by far the hardest thing I've ever done," amazed me. The guy had done a lot of interesting and frightening things. There's not a lot of room for error when you are falling out of the sky at approximately 120 miles per hour. A track is eight lanes wide, he had a guide and about the worst thing he might have to encounter is a bruised knee from tripping over his own two feet. But I didn't laugh because he was not trying to make a joke.

His comment intrigued me. I've thought a lot about it. Even though someone was giving him directions or running right next to him, I think he found it difficult because of the blindfold. He focused on the limitation of not being able to see.

We are all trying to pursue greatness. Sometimes, high achievement slips away because we focus too much on obstacles and not enough on opportunities. When we won't allow ourselves to see life's possibilities, when we focus on our restrictions instead of on our potential, all we are doing is thinking about "the blindfold."

When I started long-jumping, I had a hard time trusting my guide. The problem was not with him – he was capable, willing, and completely committed. The problem was with me. I was unwilling to put my safety in someone else's hands.

I didn't know my surroundings – I didn't know the sport very well – all I knew was I could not see and I could really get hurt. My reluctance – no, my fear – kept robbing me of potential success because I would not try.

I've always wondered how professional bull-riders knew they were good at what they do. Well, because, at some point, they climbed on top of a 1,500-pound side of beef and hung on.

Experience and the willingness to try are important. But trust holds the key to almost all achievement: trust in the process, trust in your training, trust in your abilities, and trust in others. You have to trust your teammates, your scheduler, your suppliers, and the products they manufacture. (How fast do you think a sprinter can run if all he/she worries about is, "I wonder if this shoe is going to disintegrate?")

Everyone has blind spots – every, single human being on the planet wears a blindfold at one time or another. Maybe you have suffered a loss in your family and the grief wears on you. Maybe you missed the game-winning shot the last time your teammates counted on you to make it. Maybe you made a presentation that would have secured a significant account for your company and you messed it up.

If you let those shortcomings haunt you, they will become blindfolds. If you dwell on them, I promise you will absolutely wallow in grief, you will miss every important shot, and you will never again successfully complete a presentation.

Sometimes our blindfold comes in the form of a presupposition. We assume someone views a topic the same way we do – we are "sure" that person over there thinks "this way." We live in the certainty that the answer we receive will be a resounding, "no!"

Once we figure out that everyone is different and that differences are okay, that we learn differently, that we come from divergent backgrounds, that one person loves broccoli and the guy next to him thinks it "tastes like dirt" – things do improve. To assume everyone looks at things the same way we do is simply absurd, and somewhat baffling.

We can help people remove their blindfolds by encouragement and education. On the flipside, we can accept other people's assistance as they help us remove whatever is keeping us from seeing the future with clarity and optimism.

Instead of reviling someone who is different – or even uninformed – try a little understanding. Sometimes, we run into people who have these very narrow views of life, this Earth, and what is possible. That, in turn, leads to very narrow results or a very narrow life. That makes me sad because there are so many grand opportunities, so much to see (even if you are blind), so many ways to grow and so much good to do.

Running with a blindfold may be hard. But, living successfully while wearing one is impossible.

If at First You Don't Succeed...

"Ladies and gentlemen, in preparation for landing, please fasten your seatbelts, stow all your carry-on items under the seat in front of you or in the overhead compartments. Place your tray tables and seat backs in the upright and locked position. The flight attendants will be coming through the cabin one last time to collect all remaining trash or anything you do not wish to take with you. We'll be landing shortly."

United Airlines October 2015. I was pumped.

For the last few hours, I'd been listening to an eclectic assortment of music: Adele's *Set Fire to the Rain*, John Legend's *Heaven Only Knows*, Brad Paisley's *She's Everything* – all the way to Kanye West's *Power*. Music is life.

I love music. I've been blessed with a good voice. Over the years, I've sung the national anthem at some major events: A San Diego Padres' game, the NCAA National Championship Game for Division I Women's Soccer (the Tar Heels played), the BMX Olympic Trials, and some others. Like most black kids of my generation, I stuck to hip-hop and R&B when I was younger. But I've grown to appreciate all styles and genres.

I felt the disconcerting jolt as the landing gear locked into place and the bounce when the plane settled onto the runway. We were here – Hamad International Airport in Doha, Qatar. This country was hosting the World Championships, the last, major, international event before the 2016 Paralympic Games in Rio.

The door opened, we disembarked, and hit the ground running. I had a week until the Opening Ceremonies – seven days to acclimate myself – to get my mind and body ready for action. Qatar is ten hours ahead of California – pretty good opportunity for jet lag. "They" say it takes one day for every hour's difference for your body to adjust to a time change. Following that reasoning, I was three days short.

International travel hits me pretty hard. Consider, regardless of the time of day, when I am indoors, I can't tell if the sun's out or if it's as black as the inside of a velvet bag. My body tells me what time it is – in San Diego!

Many times I sense I should be in the cafeteria explaining to my teammates why LeBron can't carry Michael Jordan's Nikes or hitting the weight room to get buff when, in reality, I'm lying in bed and listening to my roomie snoring away – lightly. After a few days, if I still haven't made the switch, I'll turn to melatonin – that usually turns off the lights in my head.

It didn't take me long to figure out that Doha is totally different from America. (I'm sharp that way.) But seriously, in Qatar, the fast food joints deliver. You call the BK Lounge and within thirty minutes, a Whopper and fries shows up at your door.

Perfect!

There was one small problem. Qatar being a Muslim country and all, no one had pork bacon. *What?* Bacon goes with everything I eat – with my eggs at breakfast – on my salad at lunch – and smothering my cheeseburger at dinner. Well, I do show some restraint. Athletes hold to pretty strict dietary plans, but I was facing the reality of no bacon on my Whopper – for over a week.

Oh, the struggles of an international athlete.

After recovering from bacon withdrawal, I spent most of my time at Suheim Bin Hamad Stadium, the venue where I was scheduled to compete. Every basketball court, every baseball diamond, every golf course, every field of competition for every imaginable sport has idiosyncrasies. The same holds true for track events.

Runways all have personalities. The acoustics of the stadiums vary (extremely important for me). Before every meet, I like to get "the lay of the land."

I'd been competing for Team USA in a number of events since 2004. But my real love was always the long-jump. Ever since Mr. Whitmer introduced me to the sport in high school, it has fascinated me.

Every long-jumper, sighted or blind, works on their approach. It is the single most important aspect of the event. It's a little like the tee shot in golf. Every aspect of the game is important, but if you hit your first shot in the woods – well – things go downhill pretty fast. If a jumper has a poor approach, chances of a successful jump are extremely limited.

One of the first things every long-jumper hears from a coach is, "Never look down at the takeoff board." Trying to catch a glimpse of the board will cause even the best jumper to break stride – it can screw up the entire approach. The idea is to run as normally and as relaxed as possible. Every jumper knows how long his/her approach takes. We measure it. We get it down to a science. When you hit your predetermined number of strides, you jump.

See – it's simple!

I figured I was ahead of the game. Since I couldn't see the board, I wasn't ever tempted to sneak a peek.

Some jumpers take off from their left leg, others from their right. Some use up to 20 strides; others, like me, prefer only 16. It really does not matter as long as you achieve maximum velocity at the time you fling yourself into the air.

Since I cannot see the takeoff board, I have someone who helps me: my "guide." When it's my turn, my guide walks with me to the line. He faces me in the correct direction (it would be bad if I suddenly bolted into the middle of the steeplechase – or worse, the landing area for the javelin), and places his right foot on the mark we have determined as my starting position. (We've measured and checked everything very carefully ahead of time.) I move my left foot forward until I touch his shoe. Then, he places his hands on my shoulders and shifts them to aim me down the runway. He jogs down to the board and gives an audible cue: "You ready?" I nod and settle into my starting position: right foot back, slight lean forward.

The PA announcer usually reminds the crowd to settle – to give every competitor a chance to hear their guides' instructions. Once the place is relatively quiet – it is a sports arena, you know, not a library – my guide says, "Turn your shoulders in-in-in. Right there."

And then, he begins. He claps his hands in rhythm and begins to yell, "Fly...fly...fly!" in time to his clapping. Yes, he is encouraging me, pumping me up. But, most importantly, he is also "showing" me where to go. I hone-in on his voice. I steer right at him.

The tempo of his calls and claps increases as I pick up speed. We're like an accomplished couple in a world-class tango contest – in tune with each other's every thought – anticipating moves before they happen. At the sixteenth step, I hear "Fly" one more time, but with a little more emphasis – a little audible kick in the pants. My adrenaline surges and, for a very brief moment, I feel like I am defying gravity.

Typically, I train Monday through Friday. I zero-in on his voice and when I take to the sky, I pray to God that I will land in the pit.

Across my Paralympic career, I've worked with three very capable guides: Brian Whitmer, Jerome Avery, and, for the last 12 years, Wesley Williams. Since working with a guide involves an extremely high level of trust, limiting turnover is a good idea.

My guide puts his life on hold. He travels with me and experiences the ups and downs of competition. He's as much a part of the action as I am. We are more than friends – Wesley is my "brother from another mother."

By the time I got to Qatar, I had been on a tear. Two months prior, I competed in Toronto in the 2015 Parapan American Games - a meet exclusively for athletes from North, South, and Central America - where I set a new Games Record (and tied the World Record) with a jump of 6.73 meters (22'1"). More importantly, Wesley and I won the gold medal.

The last World Championships resulted in a gold for "Team Lex" and Team USA, so we were determined to defend the title. In the days leading up to competition, Wesley and I spent a lot of time with my coach, Jeremy Fischer. It was the last hoorah of the year - we wanted to make a good showing.

The training sessions were outstanding. I felt strong, fast, and light - each one a key factor in reaching maximum distance. While training is not the time to fool around, we managed to squeeze in a little fun. Not everyone has the chance to ride a camel on the beach or fly across the Persian Gulf on a jet ski. Between Wesley's comedic personality and Coach Fischer's corny jokes, working together is never dull.

"Game Day" arrived - time to fly. As always, I arrived at the track a few hours before my event time. It was 9:00 AM and the temperature was already over 100° - a typical day in Qatar.

I sat in the Team USA tent and listened to *Monster* - always gets me going. I slid my headphones into my bag and put everything under my chair.

Let's do this!

Wesley and I stepped into the blazing sun and went onto the track for a few warm-up laps. As always, I jogged on Wesley's left. Our wrists and forearms always graze very slightly every so often as we make our way around the 400-meter oval. Our conversation and the occasional physical contact let me know I'm in the right place.

I heard voices – languages from all over the world: Japan, England, Australia, South Africa. Other athletes were getting ready. I was the reigning gold medalist – a marked man. No one was going to hand this thing to me.

For obvious reasons, I can't face down an opponent with a nose-to-nose, Iron Mike Tyson glare. But they can't intimidate me either, so it's all good.

We finished the laps, found a vacant spot, and I got in some really good stretching. Then, my traditional warm-up drills: high knees, butt kicks, and power skips. All the while, Wesley kept an eagle-eye and made sure I didn't get in anyone's way or anything.

My body felt good – nice and loose.

A voice from the P.A. split the sky: "Final call for Men's F11 Long-jump." That's the official Paralympic designation for my event. F stands for "field" – an event that takes place somewhere other than the track. If I'd been running the 100-meter sprint, I would have listened for T11. "T" stands for "track," the first digit identifies the athlete's disability. Blind and visually impaired competitors fall (no pun intended) under "1." The second digit indicates the severity of the disability. So, F11 means I am competing in a field event, I am visually impaired, and I have little-to-no sight. I only compete against other folks in the 11 category.

I reported to the Call Room. The check-in attendant asked to see the bibs on the front and back of my jersey. Once we were checked in, we sat for a while. Now, the voices became more familiar. I knew these guys. We'd been competing for years. I knew the guy from Spain, the one from the Ukraine, and the dude from Azerbaijan who finally showed up.

Once everyone was checked in, an attendant escorted us through the tunnel and out into the stadium. Even after all this time, I get butterflies. When I hear the crowd and feel the heat rise as we break into the sun, my insides tell me I am about to compete. Every athlete feels almost the same way, we all "feel the tingle."

The stadium embraced me like an old friend. I was in a place where I belonged, where I felt good. It was like coming home. Wesley and I sat on a bench and baked in the heat. At least I knew we were all in the same boat. Everyone was hot.

I retreated into myself, into my pre-jump cocoon, a place where I drown out all surrounding noise and every distracting, outside influence. All I hear is the voice inside my head: "I am going to run the straightest line ever. I will have my fastest approach on the runway. I'm going to soar amongst the eagles and land farther than anyone can imagine."

My focus was so sharp I could have shaved with it. I reached into my bag for my long-jump spikes and slipped them on. I tightened the laces perfectly – not loose, not too tight. They must be beyond comfortable.

Ladies and gentlemen – time for liftoff. NASA had nothing on me.

We lined up, each competitor shoulder to shoulder facing the packed stadium seats. Again, the public address voice boomed as it announced our names and the countries we represented.

"And now, introducing the 2013 World Championships Gold Medalist and 2012 Paralympic Games Silver Medalist. He is the current world-record holder. Representing the United States of America – Lex Gillette!"

A smile exploded across my face and I waved to the crowd. I was ready – I was past ready – I was in the zone.

We get three attempts, one at a time, in an order determined prior to the competition. Your best jump counts. After the first three jumps, the officials trim the field and move the top eight jumpers into the medal round. Then, we jump according to our distances – shortest jump goes first.

We get three more jumps each. Longest jump wins gold. (Interestingly, during the medal rounds, we also get to use our jumps from the preliminary round. If my second jump of the day is the longest of the competition, I win gold no matter what I do in subsequent attempts. No one said this had to make sense!)

Wesley helped me to the starting point and got me set up. Then, he jogged away. We'd done this thousands of times before.

I heard the voice from 33 meters away. "You ready?"

I nodded, put my right foot back, and settled into my start position.

"Right there." Then... "Fly! Fly! Fly!"

I took off down the runway like I'd been shot from a cannon. I locked into my strides – 13...14...15...16. I leapt, arms towards the sky like a penitent begging heaven for forgiveness. I fought against gravity as long as I could – Sir Isaac Newton always wins.

On the way down, I stretched my legs forward, hands toward my toes. When my heels hit the sand, I slid my hips as close to my feet as possible to maximize distance.

I cannot sufficiently describe the sensation of freedom I experience during those brief moments of low-level flight. It's as close to perfection as I think I will ever experience.

I did well on the first jump and well enough in the preliminary round to qualify for medal competition. The officials trimmed the field and we moved on.

This was what I'd been preparing for – the chance at another gold medal.

I lined up for my fourth attempt and heard the familiar and comforting call. "You ready?"

When Wesley began to clap, I headed in his direction at full speed. I knew Wesley would stop me if anything was wrong. He'd yell, "Stop," and as long as I had not stepped on or over the takeoff board, the attempt was not "official" and I could start over.

Wesley continued to yell, "Fly, fly, fly."

I kept on truckin'.

I hit the board and launched.

While I was in the air, I could feel my direction was a little "off" – I recognized my momentum was carrying me to the righthand side. For a split second in the air, I considered aborting the jump, but this was the World Championships and I had been jumping great. I only had three chances against the best Paralympic long-jumpers in the world.

I remembered what Wayne Gretsky said: "I miss 100% of the shots I don't take."

Suddenly, I was back in my bedroom with the Nerf goal. I could hear Woody Durham's voice narrating the action. I had the sock in my hand as the time wound down. The game was on the line.

Quit? Nope - gotta go!

I went up...up...up. Then, Gravity's grubby little hands started pulling at my tights, so I stretched forward and prepared for the landing.

I hit outside the pit[1]!

I mean all the way out - not a grain of sand anywhere. Nothing on my butt but concrete.

What's the first thing you do when you trip and fall? Do you check to determine if you are hurt? No, you pop up like, "Hey, I meant to do that," look around to make sure no one saw you, then go somewhere to mend your bruised ego (and backside).

The pain was immediate and significant, but I bounced to my feet like always. When I rubbed my bottom, I could tell I'd ripped my tights. I thought I

---

[1] If you think you can take it, check out the jump here: https://www.youtube.com/watch?v=hi3wNEyNCjk

was okay, but could not be sure until the adrenaline wore off.

My brain could not fully compute what had just happened.

For the record, it was a good jump – but when you land *a foot to the right of the target*, it does not count.

I was humiliated. Any complete analogy fails here, but I guess my mishap was like a horse leading the Kentucky Derby, then, just before crossing the finish line, swerving to the left to run across the infield.

My head exploded with questions.

Am I okay?

Where's Wesley?

Can I be disqualified for mooning the crowd?

And the big one:

What if I can't continue?

When I got back to the event tent, the officials were already conferring about my eligibility. They were not sure I should jump again.

I pleaded with them.

They reached a decision. I could stay in the competition but only if the medical officers cleared me.

I waited in the back of a sunbaked golf cart while three different people examined almost every inch of my body. Blood streamed from a gash in my elbow. I knew it was there – it started to throb once I reoriented myself. Someone cleaned and dressed the wound.

The next few minutes reminded me of my childhood when I'd waited to talk to the doctor following an exam. The news had always been bad.

I didn't like my chances.

There was good news – "You can continue."

Wesley sprinted away to get me a fresh pair of tights.

And bad news. The exam and determination had taken so long, I'd missed my fifth attempt.

Wesley was torn up. He felt responsible – and horrible. I knew he'd had a hard time watching the landing. I also knew if he could have stopped it, he would have.

I made sure he knew my faith in him was absolute.

I was a little banged up but it wasn't like I'd never hurt myself before. Wesley and I were comrades-in-arms. We were in this together for better or worse.

Every time I step onto a runway, I am fully aware that disaster lurks with every step. But the best thing a successful athlete can have is a short memory. My fourth jump was history. I was not going to let anyone in that stadium walk out with my "concrete slide" as their last memory of Lex Gillette. The competition was still "hot," so, as Shakespeare wrote, "Once more unto the breach, dear friends, once more."

Wesley asked me if I was ready to go.

I sure was, revving my internal engine like a stock car driver preparing for the Daytona 500. Everything in me screamed, "It's time to jump!" But, while the medical people deliberated, I had to stand around while my competitors made their fifth attempts.

Yes, I stood – hurt too much to sit.

So, when it was finally my turn, Wesley lined me up for my sixth and final chance. As he headed for his position, I heard a familiar voice from the stands – Coach Fischer. He yelled one word: "LOBO!"

We use the word in training. It stands for "Last One, Best One." He was right – it was now or never. There would not be another chance.

When I hit the pit, the fans erupted partly in relief, but mostly because I'd landed my longest jump of the day. Turned out to be the longest jump anyone had that afternoon.

I was, once again, the gold medal winner and world champion!

**

Adversity happens. It is a law of life just as surely as the one that says, "What goes up must come down."

When something goes wrong, it's easy to blame someone else – it's easy to point the finger. Do you know how many times the "land on my fanny" video has been shared on social media? Do you know how many comments have targeted Wesley?

Sure, my long-time friend and guide could have called me off and saved me from the embarrassment. But I could have, too. I could have scratched and preserved the skin on my bottom.

You see, there are two people participating in all of my long-jump competitions. We share disappointments, we share triumphs, we share responsibility and we share something else as well. We share trust. For a moment, let's say the entire incident was Wesley's fault, that he messed up, that he should have screamed, "No, no, no!" *Let's be very clear – I do not believe that.* But, even if it were, we'd experienced hundreds of jumps before (and hundreds since) where his confident voice guided me toward success and athletic accomplishment. Even if he bears the burden (*again - he does not*), the entire episode carries one label: a mistake.

Wesley did not aim me sideways. He did not lead me in the wrong direction. Something happened. And in the middle of an intense, high-level sports competition, two guys simultaneously decided, "Let's go!"

I trust Wesley. Every time I start down the runway, he provides the safety shield between me and disaster. I continue to have unwavering confidence in him, his intentions, and his considerable ability.

But this isn't really about Wesley and me, is it? Because we are fine. Other people, however, don't have it so lucky.

Even in the best of circumstances, something will almost always go wrong. The issue is not establishing a guarantee of infallibility. The issue lies in how we deal with one another when problems rear their ugly heads.

My dear friend of over half a decade (at the time) and I had a single, focused goal - to win the World Championship. He apologized - I accepted, changed my tights, rubbed my sore behind, jumped, and we went home with gold.

What's the important thing for you? Would you rather storm around blaming "that guy over there," or reapply your every effort to accomplishing whatever your goal may be?

To repeat: things do not always go according to plan. When everything blows up, the faster we can get back on the same page – the quicker we can "sing from the same song book" – the more success we will achieve.

Do you want to risk a lifetime goal because of an accident? Are you going to destroy a precious relationship because your feelings (or something else) got hurt?

I could have quit because I was humiliated. I could have withdrawn for medical reasons even though I had something left in the tank. How would my quitting have made Wesley feel? If I walked off because my ego was bruised and my elbow was bleeding, what would that have done to his confidence and to our friendship? Did Wesley immediately feel better the second the competition was over? Nope – he carried feelings of regret for a while.

People on the outside often assume our trust level was damaged. On the contrary, because our bond was forged in steel over time, when I toed the line for my final jump, the connection was stronger than ever.

I *knew* Wesley had my back.

And, at the end, that gold medal sure went a long way towards making everyone smile – and, eventually, forget.

The Biggest Thing

About five years ago I received an email from one of my friends, a training partner named Jamie Nieto. He outlined a non-profit organization called "Classroom Champions." It's an organization that pairs Olympians, Paralympians, and professional athletes with students in underserved schools to help them learn about pertinent life skills they can use in and outside the classroom.

I read the email.

That's nice, I thought.

I was training for the Rio Games and did not have time to devote to anything else – well, I did not *think* I had time. I smiled and went on with my business.

Six or so months later, I received a direct message on Twitter from Steve Mesler, a World Champion and Olympic Gold Medalist in the bobsled. He was a pusher for Steve Holcomb's team in the 2010 Games in Vancouver. He wanted to set up a call.

Cool.

Prior to the call, I did a little research. Turned out that Steve was the co-founder and CEO of – you guessed it – Classroom Champions.

He did not mess around. "Lex," he said, "I really would love for you to be a part of this program. I think that you have a lot to offer the children who we serve. You'll get a lot from the program, too. We want to make a difference – we want to help our kids dream big – we want them to see that they matter – we want to enrich their lives and put them in a position where they can flourish and be the best versions of themselves. You'll be a great asset. Whaddaya think?"

What kind of jerk turns that down?

I scrambled through my emails while we talked – those never have the same "kick" as a phone call. I heard the fervor in Steve's voice, the passion.

"Sure," I said. "I'd love to be a part. How can I help?"

We talked for a long time.

Classroom Champions is a year-long program. Each month is dedicated to one skill. For example, September addresses goal-setting. Oftentimes in life, goal-setting is the trampoline. Well-placed goals open windows of opportunity.

From there, we go to subjects like diversity, community, perseverance, teamwork, courage, friendship, and healthy living. We end the year on, "We are champions."

Each month, we record a three-to-five-minute video lesson on the monthly topic. We relate to the topic as athletes and, more importantly, as human beings. At the end of each lesson, we give the students a challenge – something they can work on to implement the skill into their everyday lives.

For example, when we talk about goal-setting, I tell my kids about short-term and long-term goals. At the end of the video, I may say, "All right, guys, I want you to write down what your long-term goal is for the 2019-2020 school year. Then, figure out three, short-term goals you can accomplish along the way that will help you conquer your ultimate, long-term goal."

After completing the monthly challenge, my students inform me about their activities. Some write essays, which come to me from the teacher; some create PowerPoint slides – others record a video. The entire process is pretty awesome.

I love the videos, which may sound a little weird, but everyone has their own distinctive sound. I get a really good idea of who my kiddos are just by hearing their enthusiasm and commitment. I can tell when they are "all in." Having audible feedback tells me if I am getting through. I can "see" the students just by listening to their videos.

For the 2018-2019 academic year, I had a school in Phoenix, Arizona. The teacher was Ms. Ella Maya. The class decided to create a monthly podcast called *Getting Lexified*! Each episode had a number of students from the class talking about their progress in tackling the monthly challenge. What a creative concept – and a great title, too!

I really enjoyed waking up early and listening for 20-30 minutes before I went to my training sessions. One of my favorite episodes was the November edition. My kids were stoked to inform me about the charitable work they completed for the month. November is always dedicated to "The Community." The goal is to educate the kiddos on what a community is, and how we can make our community a better place. It feels great to hear my students talk about how they adopted a senior living center and made ornaments for the residents, collected money for grocery gift cards to be distributed during the holidays, left snacks, drinks, and notes filled with words of kindness for the late-night staff responsible for cleaning the school. The kids came up with many great ideas throughout the school year. I was impressed and amazed.

Since I began with Classroom Champions in 2014, I have been sold. Now, it's a critical part of my life and I hope it will remain one for a long time. Losing my sight at eight certainly contributes to my interest. I remember the crucial role mentors played. Having someone in my corner to offer experienced guidance was huge. I received support, encouragement, and sound advice.

Some very special people stepped up for me when I was young. I could not possibly list everyone. Classroom Champions offers me the opportunity to pay back a little of the kindness and assistance I've received.

I don't want anything to happen to my kids. I don't want them to fall by the wayside or through the ever-present cracks. I have the opportunity and responsibility to work with some great young people to show them the ropes, to share my experiences, and to help them to become amazing citizens in their community, in society, and this world.

We deal with important issues in Classroom Champions. I love "Perseverance Month." We talk about life's obstacles, the inevitable challenges everyone encounters. We strive to make sure each young person is equipped to the max for the tough moments he/she will encounter.

You have to keep working, keep fighting, keep pushing, and keep trying. Keep asking questions – work to find answers. When you persevere – when you push past the problem – when you get to the top of whatever mountain you are trying to climb – Oh man, what a feeling! There's nothing better.

Victory – the sweetest taste in the world.

Classroom Champions utilizes an easy-to-use online platform where our monthly video lessons are posted. We record the lessons for our assigned classrooms. As a bonus, all Classroom Champions students and teachers can view video lessons from other athlete mentors as well. I live in San Diego, but I can have a class anywhere in the United States. We also participate in a live chat twice a year (fall and spring).

During April, Healthy Living Month, CC stages a contest. The winning classes receive visits from their athlete mentors. After working with a collection of young people for an entire school year, it's a very meaningful experience to meet them face-to-face. You already know so much about them: what they do, what they like, what sports they play. So, when you step into their classroom, the circle is complete. These very special young people become our friends. While connecting with them virtually is great, when you can sit amongst your kiddos in their classroom, it is, hands-down, one of the best moments ever!

I'll never forget my first visit. In 2014, I'd been assigned to Mrs. Jennifer Regruth's classroom in Seymour, Indiana. Her students won the April contest.

Seymour, here I come.

Classroom Champions made all the arrangements. Perhaps I figured this would be just another day of meeting some nice children and adults – I'm not sure. But, as soon as Mrs. Regruth picked me up at the airport, I knew it was going to be a special day.

I rode in the coolest limo ever: a firetruck – I mean a real firetruck, complete with lights and sirens. As soon as I heard the "woo, woo, woo, woo," I remembered the hook and ladder trucks I'd seen when I was a kid. They kept hitting the horn – you know, the special one every firetruck has.

By the time I got to the school, I was pumped.

We pulled into the Brown Elementary School drive to the sight of a mob of young people screaming. The chant started immediately. "We want Lex! We want Lex!"

When someone opened the door, I thought the roof of the firetruck was going to pop off.

"We want Lex! We want Lex!"

At that moment, the impact of what I'd been doing hit me like a punch in the chest. I could feel the smile threatening to crack my face. I was a little short of breath and I was glad I had my shades on because I did not want the kids to see the "big athlete" crying like a toddler.

"This way, Mr. Gillette." It was one of the firefighters – I'm good with voices. "You afraid of heights?"

I laughed.

"You think I know?"

He chuckled. "Good point. Well, we're going to put you in the cherry picker, if that's okay."

I'm always up for an adventure. "Let's do it," I said.

I felt the safety harness and felt the door shut.

"We want Lex! We want Lex!"

The bottom of the cage lurched a little and I could tell I was moving up - felt like a very slow elevator. I heard the shouting from below.

"We want Lex! We want Lex!"

They eventually let me down, unstrapped me, and led me into the school. The chorus kept singing the entire time.

"We want Lex! We want Lex!"

I finally got to meet Faithe - Faithe Petty - a young woman with an old soul. Throughout the year, she had written profound things to me. She stood next to me in the main office. It was her morning to make the announcements. She'd written a special introduction about me.

What she said after she finished reading made me flinch.

"Now, please rise as our special guest leads us in the Pledge of Allegiance."

I felt my throat tighten. I was thirty years old. The last time I could remember saying the Pledge, I was probably the same age as these kids.

What if I don't remember the words?

That would be great: "Lex Gillette, U.S. Paralympian: The Man Who Doesn't Know the Pledge of Allegiance."

But, as soon as I started, everything came back: "I pledge allegiance to the flag of the United States of America, and to the Republic for which it stands..."

As soon as we finished, the mayor took the mic. He made his remarks where he mentioned some of my accomplishments and talked about my involvement with Classroom Champions. Then, he said, "Boys, girls, teachers, and staff members, it gives me great pleasure to announce that, by unanimous vote of the Seymour, Indiana City Council, today is officially designated 'Lex Gillette Day.'"

I've never been more honored.

Then, the fun broke loose. The first game was tee ball. I used to play some baseball back in the day, an adapted form of the game called "Beep Ball." The ball emits a "beep" and the bases (only two in this version) "buzz," so visually-impaired kids can play "America's game."

Brown Elementary was about two buzzing bases and a beeping ball short on Beep Ball equipment, but that didn't stop us. The kids took turns lining me up and helping me orient to the tee. When I smacked it, one of them escorted me around the bases. We played in the gym. It wasn't Major League Baseball, but it was major league fun.

We spent time in the classroom talking about the year's lessons – all the things they'd studied and learned. The students asked questions – stuff we had not covered before.

I am not sure how they managed to come up with new topics. Throughout the year, we were in close contact. They already knew I had an iPhone, used a text-to-speech program called Voiceover, knew how to text, and could remember how to write my name with a pen. But they came up with fresh questions.

When we went outside to play basketball, I could tell they'd done their homework. Mrs. Regruth took my cane and tapped the rim. I was back in my bedroom in Raleigh, raining three-pointers.

Then, the kickball game. They very graciously altered the rules for me. Usually, the "pitcher" rolls the ball to the "kicker." That might have been a little challenging, so the kids let me kick it from a stand still. Once the ball was in play, the regular rules applied – except one of the students ran around the bases with me. We had a blast.

It's a day I will never forget.

Back in the classroom, the children had a huge surprise. They had all written me letters and found someone to transcribe them into braille. I read every letter. Once again, I could feel the tears welling in my eyes.

That day was a whole new experience in joy.

When the year started, Mrs. Regruth had asked her young men and women what they thought about people who are blind – how we felt and what our lives were like. You can imagine the answers.

"I bet they feel alone."

"Must be pretty scary."

"They live in the dark – pretty awful."

After a few months of working together and learning about each other, their responses changed drastically.

"I don't think there's such a thing as a disability."

"It's okay to be blind because there are so many ways to get around."

And, my favorite: "I think Lex sees with his mind."

The very first year with Classroom Champions, Google sponsored the "Giving Through Glass Program" where the company gifted a pair of Google Glass. I used Glass to give my students a first-hand look into how I train, use technology, and navigate the world. I'd wear the device and say things like, "Take photo," or "Record video," and it would happen. It would even post content to my Twitter account if I asked.

The students could go online and see whatever I posted. They watched me train and run and jump. I demonstrated how I used my computer and my cell phone. I even flew a kite and recorded the video.

Everyone in the class could see my activities. More importantly, the kids learned how to see another person's situation with empathetic eyes. They witnessed life from a totally different perspective. On a regular basis, they got to lace up my shoes and walk in them with me.

They had a window into the life of a person with a visual impairment. That was pretty cool!

I was very interested in the different things everyone saw. When I posted a picture of the track in Chula Vista, you might think all the kids would see it and say, "It's a track," but that was not the case by a long shot. If 15-20 children looked at the picture, they saw 15-20 different things – at the very least.

"I see the track and the white lines."

"Look at the grass. What's that called? The infield? It's really green."

"There are mountains in the background. Look at 'em!"

"Look at the bird up there. It's way in the distance, but I think it's huge – an eagle or something."

Different perspectives – different world views – different ways of seeing things.

I mentioned that Faithe was an old soul. Her comment reflected her wisdom. "At the end of the day, I don't see Lex as being blind because he's able to see with his heart, and when you have your heart, you have love, and love is the biggest thing."

We've lost that somewhere along the way. We live with so much hatred, so much division, so much evil, so much wrong – love seems to have limped off in the corner to recover.

The day in Seymour, Indiana had no limitations, no boundaries. No one thought or said, "You look like *this*, so you must be like *that*." Discrimination evaporated – the differences in race didn't exist. We were a tight, loving group of human beings having a good time, enjoying one another, learning from each other, and looking for understanding. The day stood as the culmination of a great year and gave testimony to what can happen when you genuinely reach out in affection and concern.

We often overlook the wisdom of youth. What's great about the young is that they simply speak the truth. They don't shade things – they have no interest in nuance. Yes, they learned a lot through their interaction with me, but I learned a lot from them as well.

When I was eight years old, the doctors told me I would never see again. But, no one ever said I could not have 20/20 vision in my mind. No medical professional can give you that – and no physical affliction can take it away.

At the end of the day at Brown Elementary School, I think everyone saw a little bit better – especially me.

All's Fair in Love... and Rio

The 2016 Paralympic Games in Rio opened on September 7. The next day, the track and field competition would begin with the long-jump. I was grateful for another opportunity to represent Team USA for the fourth consecutive time. I felt good – I felt strong – I felt ready.

The gold medal was mine for the taking.

The Paralympic Trials had been in Charlotte, NC – about one-hundred-and-seventy miles from my home in Raleigh. A lot of my family had never seen me compete, so they were perched in the Irwin Belk Complex at Johnson C. Smith University when I stepped onto the runway.

Hearing my name echo across a stadium never gets old. It reminds me of what I have been through, what I have accomplished and, most importantly, about the unfinished business ahead. Knowing that my family was in the stands gave me an extra boost during the competition. As soon as I took to the runway, the PA announcer quickly silenced the cheers. Wesley's voice rang through the stadium as I ran down the runway. Once my feet hit the sand, my family and other spectators erupted. I fouled on one of my first three, but I had leapt so far, I almost cleared the entire pit. With all of the TV cameras around, I was determined to qualify for the Games, and I wanted to put on a show in the process.

My trials performance earned me a fourth consecutive nomination to the Paralympic Games. We eventually left Charlotte and headed back to Chula Vista to prepare for what was to come in September. We had about six weeks to dial everything in before our departure from San Diego International airport. From there we flew to Houston for the pre-games activities. We went through team processing. This is a time when we have media briefings, learn the major facts about the host city, and engage in a flag etiquette session. We also learn about all of the exciting elements of the athletes' village.

Then, one of my favorite things: "outfitting." We were measured and fitted for all our gear. We got a variety of shorts, tee-shirts, tanks, polos, jackets, long-sleeve shirts and pullovers, tights, shoes, socks, flip-flops, hats, rain gear, multiple roller bags, duffle bags, backpacks, draw-string bags, sunglasses, water bottles, a team watch, and team ring.

This is not a deal where you say, "I'm an extra-large." Oh no, meticulous tailors made sure we looked spectacular in our outfits for the opening and closing ceremonies.

At the time, the Zika virus wreaked havoc in Brazil. Officials gave us the option of taking the vaccine. I did – no way was I going all the way to South America just to let some little mosquito put me in a bed for an entire week. The shot felt like I'd been stabbed with a pitchfork, but, I'm a world-class athlete, so I could handle it.

Well, I may have complained a little... and rubbed my arm. I would have preferred a Dark Knight band-aid. (I love me some superheroes) They didn't have any.

We continued to train in Houston. You can't let the Ferrari sit in the garage. You keep it ready for the race.

I had upgraded my flight to business class from Houston to Rio. I had my blanket and my pillow. It was great to recline and snooze comfortably during the ten-hour flight. Listen, when you're in economy, your food options are usually limited, but in business class? No sir. They gave me the option of four different kinds of protein; the bread they served tasted like it was fresh from the oven, and the silverware was wrapped in a cloth napkin. No plastic utensils here; I recognized the familiar sound of forks and knives hitting porcelain plates. They pull out all the stops in business class.

When my feet hit the ground in Rio, I thought, *This is what I've been training for over the last four years. I'm here. I am going to compete. I am going to win. I am going to stand at the top of the podium as the Paralympic Champion.*

No one enters a contest expecting to lose. Athletes always prepare for and anticipate victory. I'd been the silver medalist three times: 2004, 2008, and 2012. I was determined to win in Rio.

I was strong and fast. My training had been exceptional. I won gold at the 2013 and 2015 World

Championships (despite tearing my tights). I'd won gold in every competition since 2013. The Rio Games would complete the sweep.

The morning of the big day, I awoke super early, hopped in the shower, brushed my teeth, and started getting myself together. Socks, tights, the Team USA jersey, (blue with the American flag on the left side and the Nike swoosh on the right). The tights stopped just above my knees. Because of the racer-back of the jersey, I could feel the coolness of the air conditioning along my shoulder blades. It felt great.

When I put on my long sweatpants and jacket, my transformation was complete. I was Lex Gillette: Superhero. Perhaps that sounds a little corny, but when I'm just walking around, I feel like everyone else. Once I slip into my special USA uniform, I can feel the American flag on my chest – I can feel special power surge through my body.

I am ready to take on the world.

Training is long, hard, and sometimes tedious. I do the same things over and over and over, trying to strip away any flaw – working to galvanize perfection. The five seconds it takes from the far end of the runway to the sand in the pit represents years of my life. I was not going to let them down – I was not going to fail myself.

I put my jumping shoes into a backpack. The shoes look like something the Oregon Fighting Duck football team might wear – neon yellow-green. They are stylin'. And long! I wear a size 13. The strategically-placed spikes in the front half of the shoe help me grip the track – they help me fly.

I didn't eat much. I never do before competition. I eat enough to be fueled, but not enough to make me sluggish. No one wants to waddle up to the starting line feeling like they've just finished a Thanksgiving feast. The idea is to walk the fine line between satisfaction and hunger.

Wesley Williams, Coach Jeremy Fisher, and I boarded the bus for the Stadium. When we arrived, we went straight to the warm-up area. I pulled out my iPhone and hit the hip-hop. It fires me up.

Eventually, I visited with one of the chiropractors to help with getting loose. Everything needs to be in perfect alignment. After the doc got me straight, Wesley and I began our pre-jump routine.

Just like always.

I don't do the shoulder pad smashing, head-butting stuff like football players. No yelling and screaming. I ease into my "game face." I know what I can do. When I hear the call for my event, I begin to shift into competition mode.

Wesley and I chatted about some of the "good old days" – past victories and such. We spent time talking about the NFL. We're both avid fantasy footballers, so we discussed player stats, potential fantasy busts, and how our teams might fare in the upcoming season.

The warm-up is well-paced and precisely timed. No one ever says, "Okay, time to..." We ease into more dynamic stretches. I move my body into competition readiness steadily.

Back in the Team USA tent, I had someone pin on my bib number with my last name and number.

This is it, Lex. This is it. Let's go do it. Let's have some fun. Let's show the world what we've been working on, show them who's the boss of this event, show them who's the best today. Let's – win – this!

Following an announcement over the loudspeaker, we headed to the check-in tent. While officials inspected our spikes and blindfolds for conformity, I heard the same voices as always – guys against whom I've competed for years. And there are always a few new ones. Everyone has the same goal – to stand on the top level of the podium with a gold medal around our neck while our nation's anthem reverberates across the field.

Another official rooted through my bag to check for electronics. We are not allowed to have devices during competition to eliminate possible distractions and coaching. When I am running toward the pit, the only allowable "voice in my head" belongs to my guide.

The carpet in the tunnel was a little spongy. We were on our way into the stadium.

Wesley and I made it to the long-jump area without any problems. We've done this for a long time. We do things by muscle memory and habit.

Something was dramatically different today. Music blared from the loudspeakers. The PA announcer would not stop talking. I figured everyone would get quiet when it was time to jump, but the noise continued.

The number of competitors determines how many warm-up approaches you get before the event begins. Obviously, the more jumpers, the fewer opportunities. Officials like to keep things moving.

It was my time to take a warm-up.

I need auditory cues in competition. Without them, I am directionless. If I can't hear Wesley, I don't know where to go.

He lined me up - got me set, then trotted away toward the pit. If anything, the racket grew in intensity. It's customary for the PA guy to settle the crowd prior to the F11 long-jump. But this guy sounded like he was auditioning for the WWE: "Are you ready to rummmmmmm-bllllllleeeee!"

My legs locked. If I was telling myself to go, the message was not getting through to my feet. I was a little frightened. I didn't want to run into anyone - or anything.

So, I didn't go.

Wesley came back.

"You okay, Lex?"

"Feel fine, man, but I can't hear anything. Can we get the officials to back the noise down a little?"

Wesley tried. If anything, the crowd and the announcer got louder. I'd heard about how boisterous the Rio fans could be, given their love of soccer, and enthusiasm is great, but the racket interfered and I wasn't able to warm up in my usual way. But I felt good. After fourteen years, I was pretty confident in my ability to perform.

When the competition started, I was "off." My best effort was about five meters - somewhere around 17 feet. On average, I routinely hit 21 feet. I had not had a good warm-up - my timing was wonky. But I was sure I could ease into it and get in a distance that would qualify me for the medal round.

Two jumps in, I wasn't anywhere close to sniffing the podium. With one attempt remaining in the qualifying round, I knew I had to nail it.

Wesley lined me up. The crowd was still an issue. It was not as loud as it had been during the warm-up session, but not nearly as quiet as in most competitions. *Heck with it,* I thought. *Now or never.*

Frankly, it was an odd day for everyone. No one seemed to be landing big jumps. I did well enough on my third qualifying effort to move into sixth place. I was moving on to the medal round.

The gold medal was still a possibility.

I wasn't the only one struggling with the noise level. At one point, Wesley told me one of the guides turned to the stands and signaled for quiet. They booed him.

Tough crowd.

My fourth jump was still in the five-meter range – maybe a little longer. The Brazilian athlete was leading with a mark over six meters. I finally landed a good jump in the fifth round. Wesley settled me in position and headed to his spot. I heard his clapping and "Fly, fly, fly, fly!" I drove toward the board, accelerating the entire way. Like always, I jumped on the sixteenth stride.

For a moment, I was a bird, then I hit the sand.

Six meters, forty-four – a little over 21 feet. Good enough for first place.

Leading after five rounds is not as good as leading after six, but if no one beat my mark, the gold medal in the F11 long jump event would belong to Team USA.

The Brazilian jumped after me. He knew I'd knocked him out of first place. His best effort was coming. When he landed, they announced his mark: six meters, forty-three. I was in the lead by .39 inches.

I was eight jumps from the gold.

When my last turn came, I knew I had to stick one. I don't know if I'd gotten used to the conditions or if folks had quieted down a little – it didn't matter. I was ready. On my fifth attempt, I'd heard Wesley with more clarity. I timed my takeoff better.

"You ready?" Wesley's voice was perfectly audible.

I set – then took my first stride.

The farther I went down the track, the louder the crowd became. They started yelling – not booing or anything – just being rowdy. There were other events going on at the same time, but it wasn't like anyone was running the last leg of the 4x100 sprint.

Do I think anyone was trying to distract me? Was there some South American conspiracy to throw me off my game? Absolutely not. But I know what happened. And it screwed me up.

I lost Wesley for a moment – and a moment is all it takes when you are running approximately 19 miles an hour without sight.

In the middle of my approach I thought about starting over. I'm no prima donna. A restart is legal as long as your 60-second clock has not expired. But I chose to keep going; I didn't feel like I had enough real estate to pull up before I hit the takeoff board. I was dang near at full speed.

You're in it now, Lex – hit it.

I jumped.

It wasn't good.

Another five-meter effort.

I was disappointed, but I was still in the lead. I was only a few jumps away from the gold medal at the 2016 Paralympic Games in Rio.

And then there was only one jump remaining.

The Brazilian toed the line. The crowd was going crazy. Then, the strangest thing happened. I heard the PA announcer's voice: "Shhhhhhhhhhh."

The stadium suddenly sounded like the interior of the Sistine Chapel. Not so much as a cough.

When the Brazilian's guide started to call, he sounded like he was standing next to me. He could have been the only guy in the place. His voice was clear. His clapping sounded like someone smacking a block of wood with a hammer.

The crowd sucked in its collective breath when the hometown hero took to the air.

Time stood still.

I did not need to hear the announcement of the distance. The roar of the crowd told me everything I needed to know.

I'd lost by a little over three inches.

Might as well have been twelve feet.

There's nothing wrong with a silver medal. On that afternoon, I was the second-best, blind long-jumper in the world. A lot of people would do anything to be the world's second best at anything. So, I was pleased to stand on the podium. But, when the spectators joined in *Ouviram do Ipiranga as margens plácidasi*, all I could think of was how nice it would have been to hear my teammates singing with me: *O say, can you see by the dawn's early light...*

No one ever plans to finish "not first."

We go to school and want to get an "A."

We rush to the mailbox every day to see if the acceptance letter has arrived from our first pick of colleges.

When it's time to defend the dissertation, all we want to hear from the Committee is: "Congratulations, Doctor."

Home, school, work, marriage, business, whatever – we want to win.

I received a medal – one I cherish – one of which I am very proud. But I did not get the one I had intended to win.

I put on my jacket and pants and Wesley took me to the Mix Zone, the place for interviews. I talked to Lewis Johnson, a great athlete in his own right who had, at that time, covered nine Olympic Games and countless football games.

I heard the familiar voice of one of my favorite U.S. Olympic and Paralympic Committee press officers, Brianna Tammaro. She's always a joy to chat with after an event. She was gracious as always, but both she and Lewis knew how crushed I was.

The loss, if you can call it that, would not have stung so badly if I hadn't trained right – if I'd spent the months before the Games eating junk food and playing video games. But I didn't go out partying the night before the competition – I got plenty of sleep. There was not one thing I could find – and trust me, I looked – where I could say, "Okay, I need to work on *this*."

Nope, I was ready.

The questions came at me like spray from the ocean on a windy day, but I kept it together. I felt like I had let a lot of people down. I thought about my mom and my family members and how I wanted to win the gold for them. I wanted to win for my sponsors like Nike, Dick's Sporting Goods, The Hartford, Proctor & Gamble, BP, and 24-Hour Fitness. I knew the kids from Classroom Champions, my teammates, and everyone associated with Team USA had been pulling for me.

Still, I kept it together.

Until one question. Someone asked me something about my relationship with Wesley Williams. Rio marked nine years of our working together. Wesley is a fantastic guy who put his life on hold to serve as a pair of eyes for me – someone he'd never met until the day he set foot on the track with me.

"Tell me about your relationship with your guide, Wesley Williams." What do you say about your right arm? How do you explain the importance of your heart? This guy had been my rock for nearly a decade. I put my life in his hands every day. From the day we first shook hands, there was something about him – I knew I could trust him.

Without him, I would not have achieved half of the things I've done in my athletic career. By Rio, we'd shared the podium together so many times, I'd lost count. He could have been married with kids. He could have been successful in any number of different ways.

Instead, he stood at the end of a runway, clapped, and yelled, "Fly, fly, fly!" to a guy from Raleigh, North Carolina who was barreling at him on a mission to see more than most sighted people have ever imagined. Wesley is my colleague and my co-competitor. When I am running and jumping, he's right there with me. We are a team.

Most important – Wesley Williams is my brother.

Rio was our third Paralympic Games – it was the one where I *knew* we would win the gold. And, for whatever reason – an off day, bad luck, a boisterous crowd, whatever – I had failed. I felt like I'd let him down. Our dream of standing on the top step had fallen short by 8 little centimeters.

I lost it. Tears streamed down my face. Maybe some of the reporters interpreted my reaction as disappointment over not winning the gold. But my remorse came from the failure to come through for my buddy, Wesley and for all the other people who had supported and cheered for me.

I've wondered about the day in Rio a lot. The sting has lessened over the years, but it's still a little raw. Do I blame the International Paralympic Committee? No.

The crowd at the stadium? No – fans are fans – they are present to have a good time. Still, they played a role because the noise was a definite distraction. The PA announcer could have – should have – called for quiet. It is considered "standard operating procedure." The jumper from Brazil did a great job – he ran down the same track, on the same day. He made the most of his opportunity – he won.

For a long time, I thought I had a bad case of sour grapes, so I reached out to another competitor via email to determine if my perceptions were skewed. They were not. He confirmed that everyone of us jumped in a loud stadium – everyone of us except the hometown athlete.

Hey, I'm human and Rio hurt worse than landing on my backside in Qatar. But I tried to keep a sense of humor about the event. I remember talking to a reporter about coming in second. I remember exactly what I said.

"To come here, this is essentially our Super Bowl, our NBA Finals, the pinnacle of competition, and to come up just short again is disappointing. I like R&B. I guess I'm going to be playing the blues for a little bit right now."

To be clear – I got beat.

To be clear – I hated it.

To be clear – the next Paralympic Games are scheduled for 2020 in Tokyo.

To be clear – I will not forget Rio.

Where's Your Wesley?

My first guide outside of the family was Mr. Whitmer. If he had not, basically, dragged me out on the track and challenged me to jump into a *box full of sand*, I don't know where I would be today, but I guarantee I would never have competed internationally in anything. He played an enormous role in my early success – even helped me qualify for my first Paralympic Games.

As the 2003 school year drew to a close, so did my time with Mr. Whitmer. I was a senior on the track team. Mr. Whitmer and his wife brought a baby into the world. He wanted to be closer to his parents in Georgia, but he decided to finish out the year with me – what an unselfish and considerate man!

The Wake County Conference Track Meet launched my career, internationally speaking. Though my mark of 19'4" netted me a seventh-place finish, I was jumping against athletes who could see. My jump qualified me to compete in the International Blind Sports Federation World Championships in Quebec. It was my first trip outside of the United States. I was thrilled that Mr. Whitmer could go with me. When I finished with a fifth-place jump (5.99 meters/19'8"), we both counted the adventure as a success.

Mr. Whitmer departed for Georgia – he had his own life and could not very well follow me all over the country. I headed to Greenville, North Carolina to begin my freshman year at East Carolina University. For the first time since I started jumping, I did not have a guide – I did not have the luxury of a personal coach anymore. But I can never adequately express my gratitude for the gentleman who kick started my career.

Fortunately, I found someone in the ECU Exercise and Sports Science Program who was interested in helping me. Stacy Lilyquist was a fellow student who agreed to work out with me three days a week. We ran laps on the second floor of the Student Rec Center and she even assisted me during my weight lifting sessions. With the knowledge Stacy was acquiring in her program, she helped designed some workouts that kept me in really good shape.

By the spring of 2004, American athletes were regularly competing in hopes of getting nominations to the Athens Paralympic Games. Stacy was doing a great job, but I needed to compete in the long jump if I wanted any shot at making the team. Fortunately, there were a few local meets hosted by North Carolina State University where I could compete as an unattached athlete.

Guess who made the almost 400-mile drive from Cumming, Georgia to Raleigh, North Carolina? Brian Whitmer. Although we hadn't worked together in almost a year, everything fell into place almost immediately – we hardly skipped a beat. The only downside was that I hadn't been doing much long jump-specific work, so I was unsure how far I would actually leap. Turns out that I competed well, but I was unsure if my results would be enough to get me a spot.

In June of 2004, I received an email telling me I was named to the United States Paralympic Team. Wow!

While the news was spectacular, I was a little worried. I knew Mr. Whitmer could not go with me. I'm sure he would have been willing if it had been remotely possible, but he had a family and a teaching job. He simply could not take off all that time.

I needed a new guide.

Meanwhile, I competed in an exhibition race at the Olympic trials in Sacramento. At the time, Royal Mitchell was a dominant force on the Paralympic scene. He'd won a gold medal in the T13, 400-meter sprint at the 2000 Sydney Games. (He would repeat in Athens in 2004 and add gold in the 100m.) As you can tell by the "13" designation, Royal – a name befitting the "king" of the team – was visually impaired though not completely blind.

He found someone to run with me at the trials in Sacramento. (I wanted to try my hand at sprint races.)

My guide and I did fine. He was very competent, but we just weren't a good match. You know, someone can be a great caddy but simply not "the guy" for a specific golfer. There's nothing wrong with the player – there's nothing wrong with the guy on the bag. It's simply not the right fit.

When I reported to Chula Vista for our pre-Games training camp, I was still looking for a guide. I was certain I would never find another Mr. Whitmer, but I knew there had to be someone.

Little did I know that U.S. Paralympics was a step (or four) ahead of me. They had something in the works. They wanted to help me – for sure. And, like all similar groups, they wanted a medal – absolutely nothing wrong with that. I'd done pretty well. I guess they figured I was worth a little time and investment.

Marlon Shirley was another one of the 100-meter guys on the Paralympic team. Despite losing his left foot at the age of five in a lawnmower accident (and later the lower part of the same leg after a football – yes, you read that right – injury), Marlon still broke the 11-second barrier in the 100. Marlon caught wind of my need for a guide. He was buddies with a fellow named Jerome Avery.

Avery had just been eliminated in the semi-finals of the Olympic trials. He was expecting to return to Chula Vista, pack his stuff, and head home when he got a call from Marlon. I bet I've heard the story (or variations of it) a hundred times.

Marlon: Hey, man, you still want to go to Athens?

Jerome (after a significant hesitation): Oh, man, you better believe it. But wait. Am I going to compete?

Marlon (a slightly longer pause): Well...uh...about that. I don't mean with the Olympic Team – I think they're good. I mean with the Paralympic Squad.

Jerome: Huh?

Marlon: Yeah, we've got this blind long-jumper who needs a guide.

Jerome: Bro, what do I know about the long-jump?

Marlon: You interested or not?

Jerome: Well, tell me one thing, does it come with a free trip to Athens?

Jerome didn't know anything about Paralympic long-jump, but he wanted to help me. Greece sounded like fun, too, so he was in.

Jerome and I met in the cafeteria at the Olympic Training Center and hit it off immediately. I was a kid – nineteen. He was twenty-five. We liked the same music and had the same sense of humor.

He was a great guy – very vocal, very concerned about what I needed. He was, and still is, a family guy, what we call in the South "good people." We had the track and field connection – we both liked to win – and he had the burning desire to push the boundaries of greatness. I could tell we were going to be very good friends. (And we still are to this day.)

It takes a special person to be a Paralympic guide. All the athletes have some form of vision loss, but we're still very good – no, world-class – competitors. Even though I was long jumping, my training involved running workouts – a lot of sprints. Guides must be able to keep up and Avery was absolutely no slouch.

In high school, he was named MVP of his track team all four years. He ranked fifth in the state of California in the 100-meter sprint. The guy had jets on his feet.

Life takes funny turns. One minute, I was in North Carolina with the only coach/guide I'd ever known, the next, I'm in sunny, southern California working with a dude named Jerome. Over the next two weeks, Jerome and I packed in as much training as we could. Since this was his first interaction with an athlete who was blind, he had to learn and retain as much knowledge as possible. It was imperative for him to learn Mr. Whitmer's calling method.

We worked hard. Jerome and I had a lot to do in fourteen days before we shipped off to the birthplace of the Olympics.

Would I have rather had more time? In the best of worlds, absolutely. But you do what you have to do. I needed a guide, someone to help me compete. And Jerome was ready, willing, able, and very talented. You don't get invited to the Olympic Track and Field Trials just because you look good in a set of tights.

I explained what I needed – what helped me best – as a person and an athlete with a visual impairment.

"Jerome, I need you to be loud."

"I need to know where things are."

"Be very descriptive. I'd rather have too much information than not enough."

"Paint pictures in my head. Help me see what you see."

By the time we'd walked around the track a few times, he was getting the hang of it. He began to anticipate what I needed and he did not have any problem with the "loud" part.

I could hear him from a mile away, so about one-third of a football field presented no issue. I knew where he was and ran toward his voice like a hungry wolf toward a ribeye.

I was determined to do well and Jerome was onboard from the first minute. Mr. Whitmer had planted the seed; Jerome was determined to make it grow. He was accountable and genuine. He was never about himself. Everything he did was designed to make us more successful.

How could I tell he was the real deal? It was all in his voice. No, I don't have super-hearing. Forget all that stuff you've heard about blind people – the business about how we can't see, so we have highly-developed eardrums. That's nonsense. I simply depend on my hearing all the time. I've learned to listen very well. I pay very close attention to auditory input. What you read in a raised eyebrow or a smirk or a facial twitch, I can read in your inflection.

The voice will always expose the truth – and there was never a single red flag with Jerome.

We roomed together in Athens. The Olympic Village was insane! Buses to everywhere – massages on demand – there was a McDonald's in the cafeteria. Yes, I ate sensibly. I had to compete. But I made sure I dug into the fries from time to time; a nineteen-year-old can burn off the extra calories.

The first night of the Games, the place was packed. I'd always heard about "feeling the electricity in the air" – it's a real thing.

Mine was the first event on the first day – not always the case. Jerome was as nervous as I was but he stayed cool. We had a little mishap on one of the early practice runs. He was so busy booming, "Straight!" that he was a fraction late getting out of the way.

I rammed into him. I toppled into the sand pit, but Jerome crumpled. That's right, he caught a shot right in the jewels. Still, he came over to help me up.

"Man, I am sorry. My bad. You okay?"

My ankle felt a little "tweaky." It wasn't sprained but it still hurt. The trainer came over, checked me out, then wrapped my ankle.

I walked it off.

Jerome's instinct kicked in. He knew things happen in competition and he found a way to turn what could have been a disaster into something positive. When I stood, the crowd cheered; Jerome transferred the energy to me.

"That's for you, bro," he said. "That's all for you. They want you to win. They want to see you fly!"

I ate it up.

We had a few more, non-collision test runs. Then it was time for the real deal.

I felt warm and loose. My first jump was decent. My second one was really good – the best one of my entire competition: 6.24 meters (20 feet, 5.6 inches). It held up for second place.

In my first Paralympic Games, I had won the silver medal!

My mom was there, my grandma and Mr. and Mrs. Whitmer. Jerome put his hand on my shoulder and guided me through a victory lap while I waved the American flag. In the second turn, I heard a teammate yell, "Good job, Lex!"

Some things stay with you forever.

The fire was lit – my quest for gold began.

All good things come to an end, and I had to go back to the States. Back to ECU. I was only a sophomore with a lot of school work to make up because of all the time I missed on that "minor trip" to Greece. Back in Greenville, I continued working with Stacy - running those laps in the Student Recreation Center. Now that I think about it, I was lucky. I was doing very little compared to what I used to do when Mr. Whitmer was at the helm and I was still performing well enough to make international teams.

Good genes, I guess.

Ever heard of Espoo? It's the second largest city in Finland. Jerome and I reunited there for the 2005 Open European Championships.

He was also guiding a sprinter, Josiah Jamison, a visually-impaired athlete who would go on to win the gold medal in the T12 100-meter event at the 2008 Paralympic Games. Josiah was part of the Paralympic Residence Program, one of the guys who was full-time at Chula Vista. He could really scoot.

Jerome had to run with Josiah – exhausting work. Since Jerome only had to move a little when he helped me with the long-jump (he had it down pat – I never came close to running into him again), he would assist me as well and not risk being too fatigued to serve as a sprint guide.

I won a silver medal at the World Championships in Assen in the Netherlands. My jump was 6.12 meters – not as long as in Athens, but still over 20 feet.

Oh, I forgot something – one of the "I cannot believe this is happening to me" moments of my life. In the spring of 2005, Levi's signed me to be part of an international advertising campaign. The contract required me to do a photoshoot in New York City. The company said I could bring one person with me. I took my cousin, Calvin, who's two years older than I am. In our family, he goes by "Chubby," which is odd because he's not chubby at all.

The first day, Monday, April 4, I was trying on clothes and stuff, so I spent most of the time with the Levi's people. But they didn't need me again until Friday, so Chubby and I had the entire week to rip and roar through Manhattan.

How do I remember the exact date? Because the first night, we watched those University of North Carolina Tar Heels defeat the University of Illinois to capture Coach Roy Williams' first NCAA championship. What a great way for a kid from North Carolina to start off a trip to the Big Apple.

We stayed at the Chelsea, a landmark in NYC on West 23rd Street. For most of the time, there was a dog in the room across the hall. It barked all the time. Chubby heard it belonged to a famous actor. I don't want to name him, but let's just say I would have appreciated a better-trained animal.

The trip was great. The aftermath was better. One day I got a call from Jerome. He was whispering.

"Hey, man. Look, I'm in this bookstore and I'm flipping through a magazine. Guess who's in the mag posing in a pair of Levi's? You, man – you!"

I laughed out loud. Might not seem like such a big deal, but at twenty years old and to be recognized as one of the faces of an international advertising campaign. Well, let's just say, it was a little more exciting than swinging on the chain at Grandma's.

Jerome and I worked together for three years until 2007. I was very happy working with him, but the Paralympic movement was beginning to grow rapidly. We had more and more athletes – and they were faster.

I have a pretty good set of wheels, but these guys were burners. Guides must be faster than the runner with whom they work. Jerome was our fastest guide runner. His personal best in the 100m was 10.17 seconds.

This is a good time to explain Paralympic sprinting. Visually-impaired sprinters require a guide, another sprinter to whom they are tethered. Back in the day, folks used a lanyard or a shoelace. Now, the International Paralympic Committee has regulation tethers for all runners.

People talk all the time about the connection between a major league pitcher and catcher or an NFL quarterback and center, but there is no more vital connection in all sports than the one between a Paralympian and his/her guide.

Runners must stride in sync with their guides. When your left hand goes up (assuming the guide it on your left), the guide's right hand must rise. The guide runs step for step with the athlete. Talk about precision timing.

Your training is just like any other runner's, except you are coordinating your takeoff from the starting block with someone right next to you. They are there for every turn, every stride, every breath. The runners wear a blindfold – the guides do not.

The runner and guide are assigned two lanes. Throughout the entire event, the guide communicates with the runner. "Thirty meters in – fifty meters in – ninety meters – lean, lean!"

In the long-jump, guides stand in one place until the very last second when the jump takes place. In running events, guides are almost constantly on the move. The Paralympics would not exist without these dedicated and selfless athletes.

By that time, it was obvious my best skills lay in jumping. I loved working with Jerome and we already had our eyes on Beijing. Still, the Team needed sprint guides and good teammates do what is best for the whole. I always want to be a good teammate. Jerome moved over to the speed guys.

Once again, I was guideless.

I finished up at ECU in 2007 and moved to Chula Vista the following year as part of the Residency Program. The invitation had been on the table for a while, but I did not want to endure the tsunami of grief I would have gotten from my mother if I had not completed my degree.

Moving to California energized my jumping. I trained under Joachim Cruz, the Brazilian middle-distance superstar. (One of five men ever to run the 800-meters in under 1:42 and, in 1984, the first citizen of his country to win an Olympic gold medal in twenty-eight years.) My long-jump coach was Darcy Ahner, the brilliant Track and Field Coach for the Women's team at the University of California, San Diego.

My events increased to the 100 and 200-meter sprints, the triple jump, and the long jump. I needed a "dual purpose" guide. Fortunately, the world of elite track and field athletes is pretty small. Jerome "knew a guy" – someone he'd known for a long time by the name of Wesley Williams. Jerome grew up in Hanford, California; Wesley was from Visalia and had grown up admiring Jerome as the area sprinting star. They were friends from way back.

Jerome: Hey, man, I've been involved in some pretty interesting stuff recently. I'm a guide runner for athletes who are visually-impaired. It's a blast. I got to go to Athens, Finland, the UK – I'm traveling and training with these guys.

Wesley: That's pretty dope.

Jerome: If something came up, would you be interested in being a guide?

Wesley: Sure, you know I love track and field. It would be great to get back in the mix.

Jerome: Well, I have got a deal for you.

I think Wesley turned in his notice to Enterprise Rent-a-Car the same day.

Wesley possesses a quick wit and an infectious personality. Still, he is a very low-key, chill guy. He knows how to keep things light if the mood starts to tank. He and Jerome had similar qualities but Wesley wasn't as fast. His best 100-meter time was only 10.4.

A Corvette should be so slow!

Wesley and I got along immediately and have been best friends and a competitive team ever since. Across the years, we have stood by one another when there has been a death in one of our families. We've enjoyed successes like Doha and endured crushing disappointments like Rio.

We are brothers outside of blood.

Being a long jump guide is an almost invisible, job. Sure, Wesley stands at the pit and yells, "Fly, fly, fly!" but the minute I hit the sand, very few people (other than me) gives him a second thought.

Yes, we both get to stand on the podium with our hands over our hearts while the *Star-Spangled Banner* plays. But, after the ceremony, I am usually the one doing the interviews. Just about the only reporters who talk to Wesley are the ones doing deep background.

The sprint guides have it tough, too. They train just as hard. They run the same number of sprints, lift the same weights, go through the hot/cold plunges. They are as competitive as anyone else in the world.

But, at the finish line, those incredible athletes, whose desire to win burns with white-hot intensity, must back off to allow the competitor they are guiding to cross the finish line first. If a guide gets there before the Paralympian, the team is disqualified.

The whole set-up is a little like the music world. Producers grind away on arrangements and mixes and all sorts of other issues, but when the song hits the "airways," no one stands at the backstage door screaming for a producer's autograph. But the right producer can turn average talent into a superstar – and superstar talent into a legend.

I get most of the credit, but without Wesley Williams (and Jerome and Mr. Whitmer), I probably would have not accomplished very much in the athletic world.

What would the world – our contentious, fractured world – look like if more people adopted the attitudes of the men and women who serve as guides for Paralympic athletes? How much better off would we be? How much more would we accomplish as a society and culture if we all put in "the work" with the focused intent of letting someone else stand in the spotlight?

Any opportunity for achievement is accompanied by the temptation for abuse. One person's success can always lead to someone else's hurt feelings.

Yes, I am the one standing in the spotlight at the end of the competition, so it may seem natural for me to encourage someone else to act as a guide. But I am dedicated to assisting others in the same manner as I have been assisted. I obviously cannot serve as an actual Paralympic guide, but – particularly when my competition days are over – I will do everything I can to lend whatever experience or limited wisdom I have to anyone it might help.

Everyone needs a hand-up from time to time.

Where's your Wesley?

And almost everyone can, at some time, lend a hand to someone else.

How can you be a Wesley to another person?

In my sport, guides stand at the end of the runway as they clap and shout. We started off with "Straight!" Somewhere along the line, Wesley adopted "zhi" (the Mandarin equivalent).

One day, he started yelling, "Fly" (sounds a little like the Chinese word), and that has been our trademark ever since. It's also a life lesson.

Every time I hear Wesley, I am back at Crown Court, flinging myself off the ledge outside our home – and hoping I will never come down.

We all want to fly down the track. We all want to leap into the air. And when we take that jump, we all secretly hope that this time, either through our superhuman effort or some miracle, we will escape the gravitational chains that bind us, and we will take to the sky.

We will probably never actually soar like the birds, but we will come a lot closer to success if we're more like my brother Wesley.

No Need for Sight When You Have a Vision

Where would I be without my mother? A lot of children can ask the same question – and most of us would have a very similar answer – somewhere between "In really big trouble" and "Nowhere near as well off as I am today." I hope everyone feels about their mothers the way I feel about mine. She represents the primary source of my inspiration – whatever determination I exhibit, she fashioned.

Having a child who is blind is not easy. Even though Ma wrestled with her own visual impairment, she had some sight. The situation she was in certainly challenged her – if it frightened her (and what mother is not at least occasionally fearful about a child's medical condition?), she never let on. I planted my feet on the rock of her indomitable strength and decided, "We can do this."

The structure of my life is supported by the pillars of her considerable character. I leaned on her – a lot at the beginning. She hugged me, wiped the tears from my sightless eyes, dusted me off when I fell (literally or figuratively), and shooed me back into the traffic of life. She poised me for success with the same skill a championship coach positions a team; she made sure I had the training and skills to stand up to my situation, then said, "Go get 'em, son!"

My mother was tough and demanding – but she was also incredibly caring and overflowing with love. And brave.

She was with me at every doctor visit. She attended to me after every operation. While I know it killed her as the vision chart at which I peered grew blurry and eventually disappeared – when the specialist aimed the flashlight into my eyes and I struggled to tell him if it was "on" or "off" – she never wallowed in self-pity or allowed me to either.

I cried. What eight-year-old wouldn't? And she cried, too, suffering with the terrible knowledge that she could not save her son. But she never let me see the tears and while she could not stop the onset of my blindness, she was not going to let the darkness win.

One night, I wandered into the living room. Ma looked up from her prayers. "What is it, honey?"

"Ma, I can learn to read dots."

That was all it took. She knew I had accepted my situation and was ready to do something positive about it. She found someone to teach me braille – someone to help me learn about cane work. She lined up every imaginable instructor (including herself) who might give me any piece of information that could ensure my ability to live a productive and independent life.

She hoped I would go to college one day. She wanted me to pursue an education, to make friends, to build healthy relationships, and to participate in sports. She even suggested that I go on dates and find a wonderful girlfriend, someone I could enjoy spending time with. I am sure she is eagerly awaiting grandchildren (but they better not show up before a wedding!).

I can never say it enough times: Thank you, Ma!

**

Don't fall into the mis-belief that everything was smooth sailing. Every mother and son bump heads. We disagreed – I guess we probably even had fights of a sort. But, through it all, her primary interest was my wellbeing and my future life.

Particularly after I gained some mastery with my cane, she challenged me to explore, to discover, to go out into the Crown Court neighborhood, and to figure out what worked for me.

She wanted me to learn how to use my remaining senses to create mental images – to feel the changing texture of the ground under my feet – to "see" the cracks in the sidewalk – to count the stairs – to know how many steps it took from our apartment door to the dumpster or the laundry room.

I never got to play the "blind card," not once. She had a reason for wanting me to know the route to the dumpster. Taking out the trash was my responsibility. As I have already mentioned, so were a lot of other routine chores.

I can still hear her: "Elexis, you have to learn to do these things on your own because I'm not always going to be around; you need to become independent. You need to be able to survive on your own. I want to make sure that you can go into this world and into society and contribute just as much as the next person. You only make up a small population of individuals in this world; you're blind. And there are only a few people like that in comparison to all of those who can see. I want you to survive – I want you to thrive in what is, essentially, a sighted world."

Let's be honest. I was eight. And probably more frightened than I accurately recall. What kept me grounded, what kept me pushing forward, what still drives me was not *sight*, but *the vision* my mother instilled in me. She helped me understand, she taught me to believe that everything starts with an image, a belief, a dream, a vision. And once we have it, we can transform anything into reality.

What we imagine in the present, we can transform and create in the future. I slowly got it. I gradually began to "buy in." When I started seeing the possibilities, I imagined making "A's" on math tests. I began writing stories in braille.

I began to imagine.

And, in a figurative but very dynamic way, I developed my own, unique brand of sight.

Muhammad Ali once said, "The man with no imagination has no wings." Day after day, sometimes hour after hour, I developed wings. My mom helped me come to the realization that I could fly – that I could advance to a level of living beyond what I could physically see.

One of the beautiful things in life comes in knowing we can all find "the solution" even if we do not use the same "equation." I speak about the concept a lot when I talk with kids.

"Okay, you want to get to 12. How many ways can you get there? What is 3 times 4? 4 times 3? 11 plus 1? 6 times 2?"

Those are relatively standard routes.

"Ever thought about 24 divided by 2? Or 19 minus 7? What about the square root of 144?"

Same answer – every time.

We just used a different pathway to find it. First, we figured out the strategy that works best for us, then we offer it to others if it will help them along the way. The more people we can assist, the better.

As we travel through life, you and I should strive to leave something of value long after we are gone, something that can be shared by multiple individuals. Perhaps that's the true test: an authentic vision can apply to millions of people.

Consider what Chuck Palahniuk, the American novelist and freelance journalist, said: "The goal isn't to live forever. It's to create something that will."

The more I matured, the better I understood my inability to see was not such a big deal. Again, I have to point to my mom for keeping me in public school, for teaching me to make friends, for pushing me to participate and to learn alongside my friends. She helped me develop the confidence to seek, to find, and to initiate a vision.

Without overstating the obvious, if you hold a piece of paper in front of my face, I cannot see it. I don't know if it is a news article, an advertisement, or a photograph. But there are countless people around me who can tell me what is on the paper. They all belong to my vision because a vision is not meant to be a solo affair.

Let's start with someone I've already mentioned – Mr. Whitmer. It is impossible to overstate the contribution he made to my early life and career. He was my teacher, my friend, and something I have not revealed to this point. For lack of a better term, he was a "member of the fellowship." You see, Mr. Whitmer knew what he was talking about because, like me, he is visually-impaired. He has Optic Nerve Atrophy in both eyes. In every sense of the phrase, he had "been there, done that."

There are more folks.

At this phase of my life, my guide is my "right arm." He "walks with me" as I compete. He helps engineer my success. He keeps me safe. He leads me. I want to be the best long-jumper in the world. My guide has vital information I need and utilize in real time.

Coach Jeremy Fischer works on strategy with me; he sees and analyzes my technique. He knows which energy systems I need to work on, how many repetitions I need in one workout, the number of jumps I should do, the jumping drills I should employ. Box jumps? Run hills? He knows it all.

A quick aside about Coach Fischer. He trains both Paralympic and Olympic athletes. We all train together at the same time – nothing different. We feed off each other's energy; we respect everyone's talent; we push one another to make that "one perfect jump."

The strength and conditioning coaches, Sam Gardner and Gustavo Osorio, line out how much I lift and how often. They make sure I maximize my power. How many squats should I do? Do I wear a weighted vest during box jumps? How many times do I toss the medicine ball? What position do I assume for a snatch-grip lift? They work with me on executing a hang cling. They are with me for every attempt and stay right next to me until I get things just right.

My nutritionist, Liz Broad, faces a little bit of a challenge. I'm a "snacky" person – love my Doritos, Ruffles, Reese's Cups, and gummy bears. That said, I am not a problem child. I have discipline and I know what's good for me. Liz continues to design a fantastic program for me – lots of good choices in which I can hit all the major items: protein, fruits, vegetables, grains, carbs, etc. She helps guide me about what I should eat and when.

My training diet and my pre-competition diet are different. She explains everything in minute detail. She wants me to have the best fuel, the best restorative nutrition, the best supplements – everything that will boost me to ultra-high levels of performance.

Nowadays, most elite athletes have a sports psychologist. The first few times, it seems a little strange, but ultimately, I got used to it. "What's going on in your life?" "How was training today?" "How did you feel?" "Do you feel like something was holding you back? If so, where do you think that's coming from?" "What's going on in your personal life?" "How's your family doing?" "How's your relationship?"

The Hall of Fame catcher for the Yankees, Yogi Berra, is credited with saying, "Sports is 90% mental; the other half is physical." Well, the math might be a little off, but the sentiment hits the bullseye. The greatest physiological training in the world can blow a tire very fast when pierced by the ever-present nail of psychological doubt. Unpacking stuff with a sports psych – clearing out the mental and emotional attic – positions me for success.

All these people – and many, many more – stand in the circle of my vision.

When I compete, I want to win gold. Every time I step on the runway, I intend to set a record that no one will ever be able to touch. Long after I have retired, I want people to say, "That's Lex Gillette, the world record holder."

The people in my vision believe I can do it. The vision is not about ego or fame; it is about maximizing potential and achievement. I never dog it – I go flat out in every competition. The reason lies in my understanding of those who are competing with me. When I jump, every last one of those fabulous, gifted, and giving people soars through the air right alongside me.

And, my jumping is for some other people, too – people who are struggling. Whatever their circumstance or disability or pain or obstacle, I want people to see me and to *believe*, "I can do it!" (Whatever "it" is for them). I want everyone to learn to fly. I want everyone to recognize a better future. I want everyone to imagine, develop, and realize their own, unique, life-fulfilling vision.

**

One of my favorite speakers was Dr. Myles Munroe, a pastor, speaker, and businessman from the Bahamas. (I only say "was" because Dr. Munroe was killed in a plane crash in 2014. His thoughts still guide me.) After I heard one of his YouTube videos, *The Power of Vision*, I was intrigued. Dr. Munroe outlined how having a vision determines the books we read, the foods we eat, the friends we have, and the way we spend our time. His thoughts immediately resonated with me. Left to my own devices, I might sit and eat crunchy stuff all day while I listened to music. That's a little over the top, but you get my point.

I want to win gold – my vision. Therefore, I regulate my cravings for junk food and hone-in on what will help me realize my dream. I enjoy my life. The average person works in an 8-to-5 job, but I get to spend Monday through Friday, three to four hours a day (depending on the day), training to be the best. That beats sitting behind a desk or attending meetings all day.

I have great friends who keep me accountable – we all need folks like that. I even enjoy a good listen on Audible from time to time – something motivating, inspiring, or uplifting. Reading biographies of people who have shaped the world with their thoughts and actions motivates me, not just to jump farther, but also to bring my vision I have into fruition.

I refuse to be blinded by my lack of sight or limited by what other people believe I might or might not be able to do. When dealing with the realm of the possible, I am going to keep trying until it is proven I cannot do it.

What others see may not be the best for you because everyone sees through his or her own experiences. Latch on to someone who "sees beyond," someone who believes she can reach a goal if she just stretches a little more, someone who doesn't quit just because he's fallen down or failed a couple of times (or a couple of dozen).

Offer to help, to be a part of something bigger than yourself. If whatever you're attempting does not resonate with you, do something else. Staying with an enterprise for the wrong reasons – fame, money, ego, whatever – almost invariably ends in frustration and disappointment.

And be discerning about the folks who want to hop in the boat with you – I said "discerning," not "snobbish." Someone does not have to be of the same age, race, background, or education to have something valuable to offer. Conversely, some people will have a lot in common with you, but will add nothing to the journey because they are walking alongside you for the wrong reasons.

There are a lot of things "jumping in front of the screen" – worldwide conflict, injustice, division – the list continues to grow throughout history. But, in the midst of what could be despair, Dr. Munroe insisted that vision allows us to see hope even when challenges and obstacles block our view of what the world might be.

All of which brings me to my motto: "No Need for Sight When You Have a Vision®."

Though I did not create the "brand" until my adult years, that mantra has been driving me since I was eight. "No need for sight" isn't the same as "no want for sight." Blindness has been my life for a little over a quarter of a century now. There are things I would like to see, but I do not *need* to see them to press forward.

"When You Have a Vision" speaks to a connecting bridge between us. A vision gives you strength. You see what can be and maybe what ought to be. Your focus shifts away from what's in your way, to what lies beyond your current reality. Your world expands and you build connections with people and opportunities beyond anything you have previously dreamed.

Dr. Munroe often talked about "the richest place on Earth." He said it was not the bank, or Fort Knox, or the Tower Bridge (where the British Government keeps the Crown Jewels). It wasn't some fantastical place like the lost continent of Atlantis. It was the cemetery, a place containing all the people who'd died with songs still in their brains, poems still on their lips, books still in their imaginations, and dreams still in their hearts. While I see his point, that doesn't sound very rich to me.

When I die, I don't want to be part of the "Community of the Unrealized." My burning desire lies in using every chance I have to employ every skill, especially if I can help someone else along the way. And I want my vision to serve as a catalyst for other people. I want to prod, goad, inspire, cajole, incentivize, move, push, or otherwise launch them into finding their own passion and making it a reality.

The world may try to pull you down, but a vision puts helium in your shoes and will lift you towards the sky.

Helen Keller once said, "The only thing worse than being blind is having sight and no vision." I am just as human as the next person. When someone reads *No Need for Sight When You Have a Vision*® and knows something about me, I am pleased. It feels great to be recognized for my contributions and accomplishments. But, what's better, much, much better, is to learn that a young person (or an individual who was struggling) read my motto, turned his/her life around, and started sprinting down their own metaphorical runway with the intent of leaping into their dream.

Eyesight obviously did not play much of a role in my success; actualizing my vision, working hard and doing everything in my power to bring it to blossom continues to make everything possible. The principle applies to everyone, not just to blind long-jumpers. Our eyes are receptors, not determinants. Sometimes, even people with 20/20 vision miss things right in front of them. With or without sight, success comes from our ability to read our surroundings correctly, to set the course, and to go after it like our hair is on fire.

As soon as you leave this Earth, your sight is gone. But your vision can live forever.

Teach People to See

One of the perks of whatever notoriety I enjoy comes in meeting a lot of amazing people. While in San Diego for a motivational speech, I met Brian Muka, a great speaker and life coach who teaches people how to "Turn Fear into Your Very Own Super Power." He exudes positive energy and possesses a very engaging soul.

In the course of our conversation, he said some very interesting things to me including something like, "Lex, you are doing amazing things. What you said tonight hit home for me; your speech penetrated my heart. You are all about teaching people to see."

Wow, I'd never thought about my life in that way. The words stamped themselves on my brain.

When I left the doctor's office so very long ago, an eight-year-old carrying the devastating news about how my life was plunging into perpetual night, if anyone mentioned "potential," I do not remember it. I mean absolutely no disrespect to the incredibly talented medical professionals who attended me as a child. They were wonderfully attentive. Maybe my reaction came from my young mind – the focus of the conversation I remember was about how I would never see again. I do not recall anything about the possibility I might have to expand my life and, thereby, to help change the lives of others.

Fortunately, I was surrounded by another group of astonishing people who dedicated themselves to helping me "see" every aspect of life, despite my disability. My mother (in particular), my relatives, Mr. Higgins, Mr. Whitmer, and countless other fantastic people led (and sometimes pushed) me to imagine a future beyond adversity, beyond challenges, beyond the occasional scraped knee or torn pant leg, beyond the possibility of personal embarrassment, beyond missed sand pits. Some of those folks are way "in my rearview mirror" now, but the lessons they taught never leave me. I continue to benefit from the company and support of amazing people like Wesley, Jerome, my teammates, my coaches, my friends, and all the folks involved in the Paralympic movement.

The same boy who emerged from a doctor's office twenty-six years ago with news destined to send his life careening in a totally uncharted direction now travels the world, competes on an international level, and delivers keynote addresses to companies and crowds, big and small. And that same boy has one objective: To teach people to see.

If the opportunity calls for it and I'm talking at an event or visiting a classroom or chatting with someone I meet out and about, I want to convey a message of hope and potential. Yes, I may have an interesting story, but my life does not mean much if I live it only for me.

Honestly, I like being *inspirational*. But what I really want is to be *impactful*. I am not as interested in feeling good as I am in doing good. If you get only one message from this book, it would be my admonition, my urging, to be an agent of positive change. Initiate, articulate, and motivate.

We have a finite amount of time on this planet. We owe it to one another to serve as eyes, ears, noses, and minds for everyone around us. Even so-called "normal" people miss things or hear the message wrong occasionally or get lost.

Help someone! Every day! It's not easy. We have to put in the work. While I hit a pretty good mark when I tried the standing long-jump for the first time, my performance on the Presidential Physical Fitness Test did not make me a world-class jumper. It started the journey, but I had to give my fair share of sweat equity.

Some people look at my situation and imagine my life as dark, frightening, or lonely. They wonder if I hate my situation or want to change it. I never think about it. And I would not ask for things to be any different. Blindness has taught me a lot about myself and about the human spirit. Even when things are not clear, they are not necessarily invisible.

A lot of people see things and never notice them. They overlook ability, opportunity, beauty, and truth. I am living proof that you can achieve what you visualize. If I could see again, it might ruin my view on life and the world. (Frankly, there is some blessing in not seeing all of the things that are going on in the world.)

Blindness has helped me focus on important things. I know some people engage in "social media cleanses" from time to time. They step away from Twitter and Instagram and all the other platforms, so they can re-center themselves. I am not going to rage about the evils of social media. Facebook and the rest have connected a lot of people – a great thing. But, all the various opportunities to "see someone else's life" can exacerbate our own insecurities.

Not being able to see affords me the opportunity to create, see, and experience my own world. I am not disconnected from reality – I know what's going on. But, every time I awaken and set my feet on the ground at the beginning of a new day, I have a chance to shape, alter or adjust, to make the world the way I want it to be. No one would ever confuse me with Beyoncé or any other great artist, but I wrote a song once with the lyrics, "I refuse to stop building the world I can see just because nobody views it like me."

So many times, we want to accomplish something – we have an idea or a dream – but when other people do not (or cannot) support us, we grow discouraged and frustrated. A very natural, very human reaction. But, at the end of the day, I encourage you to pursue your dreams, knock down the obstacles, exceed the barriers, and push beyond the things you know and the surroundings that make you comfortable and make what you can see in your mind a reality for everyone.

They *will* see it eventually, I promise.

Blindness has opened a new world for me even when it closed the world most other people take for granted. I continue to be challenged to produce things of beauty and accomplishment – to drive beyond the physically visible and to attain the mentally possible

Actualizing dreams does not come without labor. Sometimes it extracts pain along the way, but we are not alone. There are people with whom we come in contact every day who are willing and able to clasp our hand and say, "Let's do this!"

Find them.

Engage with them.

Cooperate with them.

Stand with them at the head of that runway as you prepare to race along in hopes of taking to the air. Then...Fly!

And change the world – one jump at a time.

About the Author

Lex Gillette is a four-time Paralympic medalist, four-time world champion, and the current world record holder in the long-jump for totally blind athletes. Growing up in North Carolina, Lex attended public schools in Raleigh, then graduated from East Carolina University with a BS degree in Recreation Management. Subsequently, he earned an MBA from the University of Phoenix.

An avid musician, Lex enjoys playing his Yamaha Motif keyboards, singing, writing songs, and going to concerts. He loves movies, Nature, travel (both for competition and leisure), and finding new restaurants. When he wants to get his blood pumping a little, Lex can be found screaming his lungs out on a roller coaster.

Currently, two passions consume Lex's time – long-jumping and motivational speaking. With the 2020 Paralympic Games looming in Tokyo, Lex is focused on winning the one title that has eluded him throughout his illustrious career: Paralympic Champion.

Still, Lex loves to make time to inspire and to educate. For more information on scheduling Lex Gillette to speak at your next event, visit www.lexgillette.com – info@lexgillette.com – or call 619-600-7212.

Track and Field Accomplishments

- **2019:** *Gold medalist*, long jump (new championship record), World Para Athletics Championships, Dubai, United Arab Emirates
  Silver Medalist, long jump, Parapan American Games, Lima, Peru

- **2017:** *Gold Medalist*, long jump, World Para Athletics Championships, London, England
  Gold Medalist, long jump, U.S. Paralympic T&F National Championships, Los Angeles, California

- **2016:** *Silver Medalist*, long jump, Rio Paralympic Games, Rio de Janeiro, Brazil
  Gold Medalist, long jump, Paralympic Trials, Charlotte, North Carolina

- **2015:** *Gold medalist*, long jump, IPC Athletics World Championships, Doha, Qatar
  Gold Medalist, long jump (new meet record/ tied his existing world record), Parapan American Games, Toronto, Canada
  Gold Medalist, long jump, U.S. Paralympic T&F National Championships, Saint Paul, Minnesota

•**2014**: *Gold Medalist*, long jump, IPC Athletics Grand Prix Finals, Birmingham, England
Gold Medalist, long jump, U.S. Paralympic T&F National Championships, San Mateo, California

•**2013**: *Gold Medalist*, long jump, IPC Athletics World Championships, Lyon, France
Silver Medalist, triple jump (new area record), IPC Athletics World Championships, Lyon, France
Silver Medalist, 4x100m relay (new American record), IPC Athletics World Championships, Lyon, France
Gold Medalist, long jump, U.S. Paralympic T&F National Championships, San Antonio, Texas
Gold Medalist, triple jump, U.S. Paralympic T&F National Championships, San Antonio, Texas

•**2012**: *Silver Medalist*, long jump, London Paralympic Games, London, England

•**2011**: *Gold Medalist*, long jump (new world record), Desert Challenge Games, Mesa, Arizona
Bronze Medalist, triple jump (new American record), IPC Athletics World Championships, Christchurch, New Zealand
Bronze Medalist, 200m, IPC Athletics World Championships, Christchurch, New Zealand

Gold Medalist, long jump, U.S. Paralympic T&F National Championships, Miramar, Florida
Gold Medalist, triple jump, U.S. Paralympic T&F National Championships, Miramar, Florida
Gold Medalist, 100m, U.S. Paralympic T&F National Championships, Miramar, Florida
Gold Medalist, 200m, U.S. Paralympic T&F National Championships, Miramar, Florida

•**2010**: *Gold Medalist*, long jump, U.S. Paralympic T&F National Championships, Miramar, Florida
Gold Medalist, triple jump, U.S. Paralympic T&F National Championships, Miramar, Florida
Gold Medalist, 100m, U.S. Paralympic T&F National Championships, Miramar, Florida
Gold Medalist, 200m, U.S. Paralympic T&F National Championships, Miramar, Florida

•**2008**: *Silver Medalist*, long jump (new American record), Beijing Paralympic Games, Beijing, China
Gold Medalist, long jump, Paralympic Trials, Tempe, Arizona Gold Medalist, triple jump, Paralympic Trials, Tempe, Arizona

•**2007**: *Bronze Medalist*, long jump, Parapan American Games, Rio de Janeiro, Brazil

Gold Medalist, long jump, U.S. Paralympic T&F National Championships, Atlanta, Georgia

•**2006**: *Silver Medalist*, long jump, IPC Athletics World Championships, Assen, Netherlands *Gold Medalist*, long jump, U.S. Paralympic T&F national Championships, Atlanta, Georgia

•**2004**: *Silver Medalist*, long jump (new American record), Athens Paralympic Games, Athens, Greece